Tudor & Stuart Library
Pepys' Memoires of the
Royal Navy 1679–1688

Henry Frowde, M.A.
Publisher to the University of Oxford
London, Edinburgh, New York
and Toronto

Pepys' Memoires

Of the Royal Navy

1679–1688

Edited by

J. R. TANNER

Fellow of St. John's College
Cambridge

HASKELL HOUSE PUBLISHERS Ltd.
Publishers of Scarce Scholarly Books
NEW YORK. N. Y. 10012
1971

First Published 1906

HASKELL HOUSE PUBLISHERS Ltd.
Publishers of Scarce Scholarly Books
280 LAFAYETTE STREET
NEW YORK, N. Y. 10012

Library of Congress Catalog Card Number: 68–25260

Standard Book Number 8383-0228-9

Printed in the United States of America

INTRODUCTION

IT cannot be too often insisted upon that Pepys's *Diary* is a by-product of the life of Samuel Pepys. We are apt to forget that Pepys was not seven-and-twenty when he began it, and only six-and-thirty when the state of his eyesight compelled him to bring it to an end. But he lived to be seventy years of age, and during part of that later life he occupied an official post of the highest importance and exercised an immense influence upon naval affairs. Even during the *Diary* days, when he was only Clerk of the Acts, Monck had called him 'the right hand of the Navy'[1], and the Commission which reported in June, 1805, recognizing the durable tradition of his greatness which the period of his authority had established, spoke of him as 'a man of extraordinary knowledge in all that related to the business' of the Navy, 'of great talents, and the most indefatigable industry'.[2] The official Pepys, who thus

[1] *Diary*, iv. 400 (April 24, 1665).
[2] Wheatley, *Pepysiana*, p. 160.

appeared

appeared indispensable to his contempo-
raries, and impressed his successors with the
record of a fine career of public service, is
a different person from the Pepys of the
Diary. The work of the Navy Records
Society has recently begun to bring into
court the evidence contained in the Pepysian Library at Magdalene College, Cambridge.[1] The official correspondence of
Pepys himself during the time that he was
Secretary to the Admiralty, and other
official documents copied or carried off by
him into his own library, disclose a public
servant of a much higher type than any-
thing which the period of the Restoration
has hitherto been credited with producing.
Pepys appears here as a man of sound
judgement, of orderly business habits and
methods, of great administrative capacity
and energy, and of extraordinary shrewd-
ness and tact in dealing with men.   He
reorganized the administration of the navy
at the points where it was weakest, brought
in business principles where they had not
been hitherto effectively applied, and made
some progress, in spite of difficulties which

[1] Ed. J. R. Tanner, *A Descriptive Catalogue
of the Naval Manuscripts in the Pepysian Library*,
vols. i, ii. (Navy Records Society Publications,
vols. xxvi, xxvii.)

would

would have been the despair of a less
strenuous administrator, towards the solution
of the delicate problem of naval discipline.
The *Diary* suggests Restoration vices; the
record of the official career of its author
exhales the authentic savour of Puritan
virtues. In his unselfish devotion to duty,
in his pride in the great organization which
he controlled, in the patience and tenacity
with which he laboured to bring his sub-
ordinates gradually up to a higher standard
of conduct, Pepys is at one with the
Puritan colonels who organized and carried
through the First Dutch War. In spite
of all the tendencies of the Restoration, he
was caught up on to the same high plane
of duty. The naval administrators of the
Commonwealth had everything in their
favour—unlimited funds, the tone of the
time, a business tradition carried over from
the Cromwellian army. Samuel Pepys had
none of these things, and yet he displayed
the same spirit, and achieved no mean result.

If the intimate self-revelation of the
Diary does a good deal less than justice to
Pepys the public servant, peculiar interest
must necessarily attach to his only other ac-
knowledged work, *Memoirs relating to the
State of the Royal Navy of England*, for in
this he appears as a naval administrator
pure

pure and simple, defending an official position in official language, with the help of statistics and official documents.

In form the *Memoirs* are a fragment of history—'the contents of one chapter of a greater number, wherewith the world may some time or other be more largely entertained upon the general subject of the *Navalia* of England.'[1] We know that Pepys dallied with the notion of becoming an historian from an entry in the *Diary*, where he receives with enthusiasm the idea of writing a history of the First Dutch War, 'it being a thing I much desire, and sorts mightily with my genius'.[2] Evelyn also, in writing of his friend's death on May 26, 1703, refers both to the *Memoirs* and to the larger design of which they were intended to be the forerunner. 'This day died Mr. Sam. Pepys, a very worthy, industrious, and curious person, none in England exceeding him in knowledge of the navy. . . . Besides what he published of an account of the navy as he found and left it, he had for divers years under his hand the History of the Navy, or *Navalia* as he call'd it; but how far advanced and what will follow of his is

[1] p. 128 *infra*.
[2] *Diary*, iv. 158 (June 13, 1664).

left

left, I suppose, to his sister's son . . . .' [1]
The immediate occasion for the *Memoirs*,
however, was not historical but controversial.   A note at the end of one of the
Pepysian Manuscripts [2] tells us that they
were published about June, 1690, to defend
the Special Commission of 1686 in general,
and Sir Anthony Deane, Mr. Hewer, and
Pepys himself, in particular, against the
attacks of 'a strong combination ' 'raised
for the discrediting of the same '.

In May, 1679, Pepys had been driven
from office by the Popish Plot.   He had
been succeeded in the Secretaryship of the
Admiralty by Thomas Hayter, but with
this had been associated other and greater
changes.   The whole office of Lord High
Admiral had been placed in commission,
with the result that for five years the
higher administration of the Navy was
entirely in the hands of incompetent
and inexperienced men.   'No king,' wrote
Pepys in his private minute-book [3], 'ever
did so unaccountable thing to oblige his
people by, as to dissolve a commission of
the Admiralty then in his own hand, who
best understands the business of the sea

---

[1] Evelyn's *Diary* (edition of 1879), iii. 165.
[2] Pepysian MSS., No. 1,490, p. 73.
[3] ib., No. 2,866, *Naval Minutes*, p. 76.

of any prince the world ever had, and things never better done, and put it into hands which he knew were wholly ignorant thereof, sporting himself with their ignorance.' The result was that the effective force at sea was reduced; the ships in harbour were allowed to fall out of repair; and waste and neglect appeared in every department of the administration. In May, 1684, however, the Admiralty Commission of 1679 was revoked, the office of Lord High Admiral passed once more into the hands of the King, with the advice and assistance of James, Duke of York, and on June 10 Pepys was recalled to the office of Secretary to the Admiralty, now formally constituted for the first time by letters patent under the Great Seal.[1] The result was a new experiment in organization—the establishment of the temporary Special Commission of 1686 to remedy the disorders in the navy which had been inherited from the reign of the Admiralty Commission of 1679-84. The purpose of the *Memoirs* was on the one hand to denounce the period of mismanagement, and on the other hand to defend the Special Commission of 1686 from the charges which had been brought against it.

[1] Pepysian MSS., *Miscellanies*, xi. 226.

A

A great part of the original materials from which the *Memoirs* are compiled is to be found in the Pepysian Library at Cambridge, in a manuscript volume entitled *My Diary relating to the Commission constituted by King James the Second, Anno 1686, for the Recovery of the Navy, with a Collection of the Principal Papers incident to and conclusive of the same.*[1] Among other papers, this contains 'A Memorial and Proposition from the Secretary of the Admiralty touching the Navy', bearing date January 26, 1685–6, which was presented to King James II, 'in his new closet' (the Lord Treasurer being, present), on January 29, 'where they received it both with extraordinary instances of satisfaction and concurrence'. This 'Memorial' opens with a comparison of the state of the Navy in 1679 and in 1684, in which the figures given do not differ materially from those in the *Memoirs.*[2] Next is an account of the state of the navy in January, 1686, which is evidently the source from which the corresponding section of the *Memoirs* was compiled.[3] Then follows a 'Proposi-

---

[1] Pepysian MSS., No. 1,490.
[2] pp. 2–5 and 8–9 *infra.*
[3] pp. 13–16 *infra.*

tion

tion' containing the suggestions which Pepys had to offer for the remedy of the chargeableness of the navy, and this is the original of the document bearing the same title, which is printed below.[1] The list given in the printed volume[2] of the necessary qualifications of those who were to be employed in the work of reorganization is also borrowed from the 'Memorial', which gives a much fuller account than that of the *Memoirs* of the steps which were taken to secure the services of the famous shipwright, Sir Anthony Deane. Pepys prints in the *Memoirs*[3] a list of shipwrights from his manuscript volume, but he does not print the somewhat libellous 'characters' of the different individuals named in it, which are to be found in the MS. Of these the description of Mr. Lawrence, the master shipwright at Woolwich, may be taken as typical: 'A low-spirited, slow, and gouty man . . . illiterate and supine to the last degree.' The purpose of this list of disqualifications

[1] pp. 19–22. The form in the printed *Memoirs* is that in which the manuscript was transcribed for the use of Sir Anthony Deane and his colleagues.

[2] pp. 25–6 *infra*.

[3] pp. 29–30 *infra*.

was

was to compel the King to come to terms with Sir Anthony Deane, and the method adopted was entirely successful.

The *Memoirs* deal with four other points of interest lying outside the problem of higher naval reorganization with which they are mainly concerned. (1) The defenders of the incapable administration of 1679–84 had attributed the decay of the thirty new ships built under the Act of 1677 to 'want of care in the choice of their materials, as being built either of East Country goods, or doted and decayed English timber'.[1] In the *Memoirs*[2] Pepys, with the aid of official documents, vindicates East Country plank, and attributes the decay of the ships to 'the plain omission of the necessary and ordinary cautions used for the preserving of new-built ships'[3]— want of graving and bringing into dock; neglect to clean and air the holds, 'till I have with my own hands gathered toad-stools growing in the most considerable of them, as big as my fists'[4]; exposure 'in hot weather to the sun broiling in their buttocks and elsewhere for want of cooling with water'[5]; and 'planks not opened

---

[1] Pepysian MSS., *Admiralty Letters*, X. 170.
[2] pp. 33–54 *infra*.   [3] p. 47 *infra*.
[4] ib. *infra*.   [5] p. 48 *infra*.

†   upon

upon the first discovery of their decays, nor pieces put in where defective '.[1] (2) The *Memoirs*[2] print, presumably from the Pepysian MSS.,[3] James II's 'establishment about plate carriage and allowance for captains' tables ', dated July 15, 1686—an attempt to revive discipline in the navy by giving the Admiralty a ready control over ships on foreign service, and at the same time so to improve the position of the captains as to put them beyond the reach of temptations to neglect public duty for private gain. (3) Pepys attempts a financial vindication of the Special Commission of 1686,[4] showing that the sums expended by it amounted altogether to £307,570 less than 'might unexceptionally have been expended' on the calculation of the original 'Proposition '; and notes that the salaries of the officials who effected this saving amounted to little more than £6,000 and the 'simple wages of a worn, unassisted secretary '.[5] (4) From the ample materials at his disposal he furnishes complete and orderly lists of the ships of the Royal Navy.[6] Some of this

---

[1] p. 48 *infra*.   [2] pp. 55–68 *infra*.
[3] No. 2,867, *Naval Precedents*, p. 245.
[4] pp. 80–5 *infra*.
[5] p. 85 *infra*.   [6] pp. 86–127 *infra*.

information

information was probably derived from his *Register of the Ships of the Royal Navy of England* now preserved in the Pepysian Library.[1]

Regarded as controversial literature, Pepys's *Memoirs* are extraordinarily methodical, temperate, and fair. The official documents are allowed to tell their own story; where they are condensed, our access to the original materials enables us to appreciate the skill, accuracy,[2] judgement, and sense of proportion with which the condensation is effected; and the writer contrives to preserve throughout a tone of reasonableness which was not any too common in the controversies of the day. Moreover the conclusions to which Pepys came are confirmed ·from independent

[1] Pepysian MSS., no. 2,940. The *Register* is printed in the *Descriptive Catalogue of the Naval Manuscripts in the Pepysian Library*, vol. 1. (Navy Records Society Publications, vol. xxvi.)

[2] It is curious that Pepys, usually so accurate, should begin his *Memoirs* with a mistake. He speaks of himself (p. 1 *infra*) as 'now shut up in the Tower' in *April*, 1679. As a matter of fact he was not committed thither under the Speaker's Warrant until May 22 (*D. N. B.* xliv. 363). The last letter written by him as Secretary to the Admiralty is dated May 21 (Pepysian MSS., *Admiralty Letters*, ix. 284).

sources

sources. His condemnation of the administrators of 1679-84 is supported, as Macaulay points out,[1] by an expert from the French Admiralty; and his eulogy of the Special Commission of 1686 is justified by the report of the Commission of Public Accounts appointed in December, 1690,[2] under an Act passed in the first Parliament of William III.

In his concluding remarks [3] Pepys ascends for a moment from the plane of polemics to higher ground. The essential 'truths' of the 'Sea Œconomy' of England are as valid to-day as when he stated them more than two centuries ago—'that integrity and general (but unpractised) knowledge are not alone sufficient to conduct and support a navy so as to prevent its declension into a state little less unhappy than the worst that can befall it under the want of both': 'that not much more (neither) is to be depended on, even from experience alone and integrity, unaccompanied with vigour of application, assiduity, affection, strictness of discipline, and method'; but that what is needed above

[1] *History of England* (Longmans, 2 vols., 1880), i. 146.
[2] Dec. 26, 1690 (*Commons Journals*, x. 528).
[3] pp. 128–31 *infra*.

all

all things is 'a strenuous conjunction of all
these '. And the *non nobis* with which he
concludes his volume is not inconsistent
with that sober Puritanism upon which
this complex character was ultimately
based—'and yet not such but that (even
at this its zenith)' the navy of England
'both did and suffered sufficient to teach
us that there is Something above both
that and us that governs the world. To
which (Incomprehensible) alone be glory.'

A correspondence on the bibliography of
the *Memoirs* has been published in *Notes
and Queries,*[1] from which it appears that
some copies of the original edition contain
manuscript corrections, apparently made at
the same time and with the same ink and pen.
These have been attributed to Pepys himself, and may very well have been made
by him in the copies which he gave away

[1] *Seventh Series,* vol. vii, pp. 81, 196, 274,
315, 398. The writer of this Introduction
desires to acknowledge his indebtedness for this
reference to Mr. C. E. Doble of the Clarendon
Press, who has also allowed him to see a copy
of the *Memoirs* containing Pepys's corrections.

b among

among his friends. They have all been noted in the reprinted text.[1]

Although some of the corrections suggest that the author might have read his proofs more carefully in the first instance,[2] yet if they are taken as a whole, another inference may be drawn from them. Provided that the identification of the handwriting is correct, they show the characteristic care which Pepys afterwards took to make his defence of his naval administration accurate on points of form, as well as in all matters of detail.

J. R. TANNER.

St. John's College, Cambridge,
April, 1906.

[1] pp. 7, 19, 21, 22, 23, 24, 32, 39, 49, 50, 56, 65, and 76 *infra.*

[2] *Cf.* also the misprint for 'particularly' on p. 50 *infra,* line 16.

𝕸𝖊𝖒𝖔𝖎𝖗𝖊𝖘

Relating to the

S T A T E

O F T H E

ROYAL NAVY

O F

E N G L A N D,

For Ten Years, Determin'd *December* 1688.

Quantis moleſtiis vacant, qui nihil omninò cum Populo contrahunt ? Quid Dulcius Otio Litterato ? Cic. Tuſc. Diſp.

L O N D O N.

Printed for *Ben. Griffin,* and are to be ſold by *Sam. Keble* at the Great *Turks-Head* in *Fleet-ſtreet* over againſt *Fetter-Lane,* 1690.

𝕸𝖊𝖒𝖔𝖎𝖗𝖊𝖘

Relating to the

STATE

OF THE

ROYAL NAVY

OF

ENGLAND.

'TWas in *April* 1679, when (my unhappy *Master*, his then *Royal Highness,* having but newly been commanded abroad, and my self now shut up in the *Tower*) His *Majesty* K. *Charles the Second* was led to the exchanging the *Method*, wherein the *Affairs* of his *Admiralty* had for some years before been manag'd under his own Inspection, for that of a *Commission*, charg'd with the *Execution* of the whole *Office* of his *High Admiral.*

April 1679

Admiralty-Management altered.

An

The Jun-
cture pro-
per for
the Alte-
ration.

An *Occurrence* carrying this in it of peculiar; That no one *Article* of *Time* appears within the whole *Hiſtory* of our *Navy*, wherein this could have fallen out more equally towards the *Perſons* immediately intereſted in the *Alteration.* Foraſmuch as (by occaſion of a *War* then newly in agitation with *France*) the *State* of the *Navy*

Inquiſi-
tion into
the Navy
by Par-
liament.

had paſt an *Inquiſition* ſo publick and ſolemn (extant at this day in the *Regiſters* both of *Parliament* and its own) as no time can ſhew to have at once been ever before taken; leaving no room for Controverſie (under any future *Events*) touching the condition wherein the *Navy* was at that time, either deliver'd over by the *one*, or taken in charge by the *other*.

State of
the Navy
then.

Which Condition *was ſhortly this*, viz.

Ships in
Sea-Ser-
vice.

I. The *Groſs* of the *Fleet* of *England* was in that ſtate of *Repair*, as (in proſpect of the foremention'd *War*) to have had but few Months before, and upon leſs than four Months warning,

ing, actually in *Sea-fervice* and *Pay*, compleatly furnifhed with fix Months *Sea-ftores, Eighty three* of His *Majefties* own *Ships* of *War* and *Fire-Ships* (over and above Merchant-men, and the numerous Train of *Ketches, Smacks, Yachts,* and other fmall Craft, attending the fame) and thefe of the higheft, as well as other Rates, employing in the whole above 18000 Men, as follows.

𝕬𝖇𝖋𝖙𝖗𝖆𝖈𝖙 *of the* 𝕱𝖑𝖊𝖊𝖙 *in* Auguft, 1678.

		Nº	Men.
	1	5	3135
	2	4	1555
Rates	3	16	5010
	4	33	6460
	5	12	1400
	6	7	423
Fire-Ships		6	340

Total 83 — 18323

Of which were left in like *Sea-Pay* at the time of my *Confinement,* Three-

fcore

ſcore and Sixteen of the following
Rates, bearing 12000 Men.

𝕬𝖇𝖋𝖙𝖗𝖆𝖈𝖙 *of the* **𝕱𝖑𝖊𝖊𝖙,** *left by Mr.*
Pepys *in* Sea-pay, April 1679.

$$N^o$$

$$Rates \begin{cases} 1 \longrightarrow 1 \\ 2 \longrightarrow 3 \\ 3 \longrightarrow 15 \\ 4 \longrightarrow 30 \\ 5 \longrightarrow 12 \\ 6 \longrightarrow 7 \end{cases} \quad \begin{matrix} Men. \\ -12040 \end{matrix}$$

Fire-Ships ——— 8

Total 76

Condition of thoſe in Harbour.   II. The whole *Reſidue* of the *King's* Repairable *Ships* were (upon no leſs ſolemn an *Enquiry*) reported within the ſame time, by the *Surveyor* of his *Navy,* and *Body* of the *Navy-Board,* in a condition of being throughly fitted for the *Sea* and furniſh'd with *Sea-ſtores* for 50000 *l.*

Stores in Maga-zine.   III. And towards this, and the anſwering what extraordinary *Supplies*

this

this *Fleet* (had not the War prov'd abortive, and the *Ships* with their *Stores* been thereby in the main foon brought in and laid up) might have had occafion for, beyond its fore-mention'd fix Months; a further *Re-ferve* remain'd untoucht in *Magazine*, to the value of *Threefcore thoufand pounds.*

IV. Laftly, A *Force* additional to all this of Thirty *Capital Ships* was then actually in *Building*; Whereof Eleven newly *Launch'd*, and the Re-mainder (all of them) under an affidu-ous profecution upon the *Stocks.* An Addition, rendering the *Whole* a Se-curity not unequal (ordinary *Providence* concurring) to the publick *Ends* of it, in the maintenance of the *Peace* and *Honour* of the *Government* on *Shore*, and fupport of its ancient, rightful, and envy'd *Title* to *Dominion* at *Sea*. *Thirty Capital Ships in Building.*

This was the *Pofture* of the *Royal Navy* at the time of my *Removal* from it. Concerning which I fhall take
the

the liberty only to fay, That though I am one, who could never think any room left for a *Subject's* Supererogating in the honeft *Service* of his *Prince*; yet cannot I but own fo much content in the contemplation of that little *Part* I had born in the rendring it

State of the Navy of England in no time better.

fuch, as may reafonably arife from the not being confcious of any one *Inftance* to be fhewn me through the whole *Marine Hiftory* of *England*, of a time wherein its *Navy* had been ever before recorded in a better.

May 1679, Commiffion of the Admiralty, its Date and Duration.

𝕬𝖓𝖉 fo fets out this *Commiffion* in *May* 1679, continuing in its Execution five years.

During which, being my felf wholly fequeftred from that and all other *Publick Affairs*, Thofe of the *Navy* became foreign to me; as having no other Notices concerning them, than what too often occurr'd in common converfation, touching the *effects* of

Conduct thereof obferved.

Inexperience daily difcovering themfelves in their *Conduct*; and (what was no mean *Addition* to it) the unconcernment

ment wherewith his then *Majefty* was faid to fuffer his being familiarly entertain'd on that Subject; while at the fame time his tranfcendent *Maftery* in all *Maritime* [1] *Knowledge*, could not (upon the leaft *Reflection*) but bring into his view, the ferious *Reckoning* the fame muft foon or late end in, to his *Purfe* and *Government.* As at the five *years* end it prov'd to do.

When (in *May* 1684.) being felf-convinc'd of the inexpediency of his longer continuing the *Navy* under that *Management*, He was pleas'd to come to a fudden determination, of refuming the Bufinefs of it into his own *Hands*, affifted by his *Royal Brother* then come back, and by his Commands, (neither fought-for, nor forefeen, but brought me exprefly from *Windfor* by the Lord *Dartmouth*) to require my immediate Return to the *Poft* I had formerly had the *Honour* of ferving him at, therein.

Purfuant hereto, the late *Commiffion* being

May 1684.

Navy refumed into the Kings own hands, affifted by his R.H.

Mr. Pepys recalled.

Admi-raltyCom-miffion diffolved.

[1] *Maritine corr.* S. P.

A Re-
view of
the Navy
as re-
turned to
the King,
here Sta-
ted.
being diſſolv'd, and His *Majeſty* taking
to himſelf the Perſonal *Direction* of
its *Work*; He judg'd it for his *Service*
to begin with a freſh *Enquiry* into the
Condition wherein his *Navy* was now
return'd him, and found the *Reſult* of
it this.

Ships at
Sea.
I. *Four and Twenty* of his *Ships* (and
no more) were then at *Sea*, and thoſe
of the following *Rates* (not one above
a fourth) employing but 3070 *Men*.

Abſtract *of the* **Fleet** *at* Sea *at the*
Cloſe *of the* Commiſſion *of the*
Admiralty, May 1684.

		N°.	Men.
Rates—	4ᵗʰ.——12——		2120
	5 —— 5——		560
	6 —— 5——		325
Fire Ships	—— 2——		65

Total 24——3070

Condition
of thoſe
in Har-
bour.
II. The *Remainder* of the *Navy* in
Harbour ſo far out of *Repair*, as to
have had the *Charge* of that alone
(without *Sea-Stores*) eſtimated juſt before

fore by the same *Surveyor* and *Board*, at no less than *One hundred and twenty thousand Pounds.*

III. And towards this, a *Magazine* of *Stores,* as lately reported from the same *Hands,* not to amount to *Five thousand Pounds.*

Maga-zine.

A *Magazine,* so unequal to the Occasions of such a *Navy;* that whereas *Peace* us'd evermore to be improv'd to the making up the *wasteful effects* of *War.* This appears (after the longest *Vacation* of a *Home-marine Peace,* from the *Restauration* of the *King* to this *Day*) to have brought the *Navy* into a *state,* more deplorable in its *Ships,* and less relievable from its *Stores,* than can be shewn to have happen'd (either in the *One,* or the *Other*) at the *Close* of the most expenceful *War,* within all that time, or in *forty years* before.

That Maga-zine con-sidered.

IV. *Especially,* when in this its *General* ill plight, consideration shall be had of that *Particular* therein, which relates to the *Thirty New Ships.* Not more

Ill State of the 30 New Ships.

more furprizing for the *Fact*, (after
the folemnity and amplenefs of the
Provifion made for them by *Parliament*)
than important for its *Confequences.*

Import of thofe Ships. Forafmuch as in thefe Ships refted
not only that, by which the prefent
Sea-ftrength of *England* furmounted all
it had ever before had to pretend to,
and the utmoft that its prefent *Woods*
(at leaft within any reafonable *Reach*
of its *Arfenals*) feem now able to fupport with *Materials*, or its *Navigation*
with *Men*; but that *Portion* alfo of
the fame, upon which alone may at
this day be rightfully faid to reft, the
virtue of the *whole*, oppos'd to the no
lefs confiderable *Growths* in the *Naval
ftrengths* of *France* and *Holland.*

The ill-nefs of their State par-ticular-ized. The greateft part neverthelefs of
thefe *Thirty Ships* (without having ever
yet lookt out of *Harbour*) were let to
fink into fuch Diftrefs, through *Decays*
contracted in their *Buttocks, Quarters,
Bows, Thick-ftuff* without *Board*, and
Spir-kettings upon their *Gun-decks* within; their *Buttock-Planks* fome of them
ftarted

started from their *Tranfums*, *Tree-nails*
burnt and rotted, and *Planks* thereby
become ready to drop into the *Water*,
as being (with their Neighbouring
Timbers) in many places perifh'd to
powder, to the rendring them unable
with fafety to admit of being *breem'd*,
for fear of taking *Fire*; and their
whole *fides* more difguis'd by *Shot-
boards* nail'd, and *Plaifters* of *Cunvas*
pitch'd thereon (for hiding their *Defects*, and keeping them above *Water*)
than has been ufually feen upon the
coming in of a *Fleet* after a *Battle*;
that feveral of them had been newly
reported by the *Navy-Board* it felf, to
lye in danger of *finking* at their very
Moorings.

And *this*, notwithftanding above *Exceffive*
Six hundred thoufand pounds (not yet *Charge*
accounted for by the *Navy-Board*) *of thefe*
Ships, un-
fpent in their *Building* and *Furniture*, *accounted*
with above *Threefcore and ten thoufand* *for.*
pounds more demanded for compleating them, amounting together to
6 70000 *l.*; and therein *exceeding*, not
only

only the *Navy Officers* own *Eſtimates*,
and their *Maſter-Ship-wrights Demands*,
but even the *Charge* which ſome of
them appear'd to have been actually
built for, by above *One hundred* and
ſeventy thouſand pounds.

The Fond   And notwithſtanding too, the flow-
for them ing in of the *Monies* provided for
well an- them by *Parliament*, faſter (for the
ſwered. moſt part) than their *Occaſions* of
employing it.

Provi-   In a word ; notwithſtanding the
ſions for *ſtrict Proviſion* made by *Parliament*,
ſecuring the repeated *Injunctions* of His *Majeſty*,
an Ac-
count of the *Orders* of the then *Lord Treaſurer*,
theſe and ampleneſs of the *Helps* purpoſely
Ships, yet allow'd (to the full of their own
ineffectu-
al.   *Demands and Undertakings*) for ſecuring
a ſatisfactory *Account* of the *Charge*
and *Built* of the ſaid *Ships*.

400000l. V. *Laſtly*, While the *Navy* (under
per An- this five *years* uninterrupted *Peace*)
num paid was ſuffer'd to ſink into this calamitous
the Navy
all this eſtate, even to the rendring ſome of
while. its *Number* wholly *irreparable*, and
reducing others (the moſt conſiderable

in

in *Quality*) to a *Condition* of being with difficulty kept above *Water*; the *Navy* (as His *Majefty* was then affur'd by the *Lord Treafurer*) had been all that while fupply'd, (one year with another) with *Four hundred thoufand Pounds* per Ann.

Which being then the *Condition* of the *Navy*, and (as fuch) not receptive of any fenfible *Amendment* within the fhort remainder of the *Life* of *King Charles*; his *Royal Brother* King *James* (upon his coming to the *Throne* in *February* following) was pleas'd to take among the firft of his Cares this of the *Navy*, by an immediate application to the animating and enabling its *Officers* (with fuitable Supplies of *Money*) to an induftrious and effectual *beftirring* themfelves towards the *redreffing it*. *Death of K. Charles, Febr.* 1684. *K. James falls immediately upon the redrefs of the Navy, by the Officers thereof.*

But with fuch unfuccefsfulnefs (after a whole *year's* Proof of their *Performances*) as upon a frefh *View* of its *State*, taken in *January* 168⅚, to difcover it felf ftill declin'd to a yet more *But after a years proof wholly unfuccefsful.*

deplor-

State of the Na-vy, January, 1685. deplorable degree of *Calamity*; as follows,

I. After the *Expence* in *Workmanſhip* and *Materials* of above *Ninety thouſand Pounds*, the *Navy-Officers* ſtill demand

90000 *l. ſpent fruitleſly.* for the *Repairs* of the *Fleet* the very ſame *Sum* the *Works* had by themſelves been valu'd at, before a *Penny* of that *Ninety thouſand pounds* had been laid out.

Ships not Graved. II. Not a *Quarter* of the *Ships* grav'd, which *themſelves* had propos'd the having done within that time, and been expreſly ſupply'd with the *Monies* demanded for it.

No Ships in preſent readineſs for Ser-vice upon an Exi-gence. III. But one fourth *Rate*, and not ſo much as one *Fifth*, found (in the *Exigence* of the *Duke* of *Monmouth*'s *Invaſion*) in a condition of being got to *Sea*, in leſs than two *Months*, but by robbing of the very *Harbour-Guard.*

The 30 *New Ships not yet gone in hand with,* IV. Several of the 30 *Ships* (re-ported near two years ſince in a condition of *ſinking*) not yet ſo much as gone in hand with, though *Money* ex-

exprefly fupply'd for that ufe too, by
the Lord Treafurer.

V. Their *Stores* alfo of greateft
value, and calling for moft time to
provide (fuch as *Cables*, *Sails*, &c.) fo
much wanting, either through *Decay*,
or being (in neglect of the *Statute*)
diverted to *other ufes*, as not to have
any one of them furnifh'd for the
Sea, had they been otherwife in *Condition* for it.

VI. *Twice* as much time now demanded for fitting out *forty two* Ships,
as had a year and half fince been
ask'd for *fifty five*.

VII. Not the leaft *Provifion* made
of *Long Timber* or *Plank*, for anfwering the moft preffing and weighty
works of the *Growing year*; though
the greateft Part of the *Money* demanded for that ufe alfo, had been
actually *advanc'd*, and the *Refidue* lay
in a known readinefs to be fo, as faft
as call'd for.

VIII. *Three Years* ftill infifted on
for the *Repair* of the *Fleet*, while *five*
Months

*Though
Money
fupply'd.*

*Their
Stores al-
fo want-
ing.*

*The Time
asked for
fitting out
Ships,
more than
doubled.*

*No Pro-
vifion
made of
the moft
neceffary
Materi-
als,
though
Money
fupply'd
for that
alfo.*

*Time
length-*

*ened be-
yond
measure
for repair
of the
Fleet.*

Months only refted unexpir'd of the time, within which (by former *Calculations* of their own) the *whole* was to have been *finifh'd.*

*Notwith-
ftanding
all Helps,
the Fleets
decays
outgrow
their
Cure.*

IX. *Laftly,* After the utmoft *proofs* of the *Procedures* of this *Board,* affifted by *Money* to the height of their *Demands,* it feem'd manifeft to *His Majefty,* that the *Fleet's Decays* outgrew their *Cure;* and that fhould no other *courfe* be found for the remedying it, than what was now *ftirring* among the *Navy Officers* (whofe *Eftimates* of the very fame *date* were found fometimes to differ not lefs than *double,* nay even *treble,* in the *Charge* of the *Repairs* of the very fame *Ship*) no time could be affign'd, within which (if ever) their *Decays* (even as they then ftood, without ought allow'd for their greatnings by *Delay*) could have their *Repairs* depended on.

*Navy
Officers
Eftimates
of Repairs
incon-
fiftent.*

*Nor any
time to be
depended
on for the
difpatch
thereof.*

*Caufes of
thefe
Evils
what,
and what
not.*

From whence, and from the *King's* being in an efpecial manner convinc'd, that no part of thefe *Evils* fprang from the want of *Money, Hands, Materials*

or

or *Time*, but from other *Imperfections*, obvious enough, but uneasie to be now rectify'd in the *Persons* principally accountable for them ; and considering likewise the necessity of having some instant and effectual *Remedy* provided, e're the *mischiefs* attending this *Management* became (what *one years* delay more must, at least as to the New Ships, have render'd them) insuperable : He was pleas'd (in subserviency to his own) to require my *Thoughts* touching the *Methods* most likely to compass his *Royal Aim* herein, and how far that (with the other standing and indispensable *Charges* of his *Navy* at *Sea* and in *Harbour*) might be together answer'd with 400000 *l. per Annum* ; the Sum the then *Lord Treasurer* first proposed the way of providing, and the *King* his Readiness to have set entirely apart for it.

Which accordingly I soon after presented him with, in the *Terms* following.

Some instant Remedy necessary.

To be (with the other necessary charges of the Navy) defrayed with 400000l. per Ann.

To

To the *KING*.

Sir,

THough the general and habitual ſupineſs, waſtefulneſs *and* neglect *of* Order *univerſally ſpread through your whole* Navy, with the No-proviſion *yet made of Materials the moſt neceſſary and difficult to be found for this ſo great* Work; *adding thereto the impoſſibility of arriving at any perfect knowledge of the* weight *of that* work, *from the diſagreements daily diſcovered between the* Eſtimates *and real* Charge *of* Works *when perform'd; and laſtly, the heavy conſequences of any* Failure *that may happen in its Execution, ſeem to render any peremptory* undertaking *herein (from* me *at leaſt) very unſafe, if at all juſtifiable. Yet ſo much am I acquainted with the Power of* Induſtry *and* Good Husbandry, *joyn'd with* Knowledg *and* Methodical Application *(no two of which ſeem at this day ſtirring together in any Part of your* Naval Service) *that after weighing every Article of what I am by your* Majeſty's *Com-*

Tender of undertaking ought.

Command now going to offer you, I am satisfy'd that your Majefty *may reafonably expect the fervices mention'd in the following* Propofition, *Viz.*

Propofition.

𝕿𝖍𝖆𝖙 *with* 400000 l. per Annum, *fupply'd by* 100000 *l. within each* Quarter, *and in a known and effectual* Order *of* Payments, *to be pre-adjufted with the* Perfons, *who (being rightly* [1] *qualify'd for it) fhall be intrufted by your* Majefty, *with the* Management *thereof, and affifted with your* Authority *in all matters conducing to the* Recovery *of the loft* Difcipline *and* Induftry *of your* Navy; *the* Retrenchment *of all unneceffary* Charges *and* Waftes; *the encouraging and improving all means of* Good Husbandry *and reafonable* favings; *and the due* Correction *of all* mifdoers *in any of the* Premiffes; *your* Majefty *may expect the* Effects *following,* Viz.

I. *The whole* ordinary charge *of* your Navy *on* Shore *and in* Harbour *to be fully defray'd, and therein the* Hulls

Mr. Pepys's Propofition.

400000*l.* the Fund affign'd for it, with the conditions of the Propofition.

Ordinary charge and works

[1] *rightfully corr.* S. P.

C 2

Hulls *of your* Ships *duly kept in their*
ordinary Repair, *grav'd* (*as by the*
Rules *of the* Navy *they ought always
to have been*) *by one* Third *every* year,
and supply'd with Ground Tackle *fufficient for their fafe* mooring; *and your*
Offices *alfo and* dwelling Houfes, Store-
Houfes, Wharfes, Cranes, *and* Keys *to
be throughout put into, and kept in their*
Ordinary repair.

*Extra-
ordinary
Repairs
defcribed.*
II. The extraordinary Decays *under
which the* Body *of your whole* Fleet *in*
Harbour *now lies, to receive the full of
their* Repair *alfo, to the utmoft of what
has been yet difcover'd and defcribed in
the laft and higheft* Surveys *and* Eftimates
prefented of them to your Majefty *by your*
        Navy Officers, *amounting*

	l.
Repaires —	132000
Sea-Stores-	88000
Tot —	220000

(*with their* Stores) *to* 220000*l.*;
and this (*with the finifhing
the* Three New 4*th.* Rates)
to be compleated *within the* year

*Within
what
time, and
how to
be per-
formed.*
1688.; *and fo done, that your* Majefty
and your Lord Treafurer *may* (*according
to the ancient and rightf*▪ Methods *of
the* Navy) *be fatisfy'd at the end of each*
                         fer-

fervice, *how the* Charge *thereof has concurr'd with, exceeded, or fallen fhort of their* Eftimates, *and the* Monies *fav'd there-from be made good to your* Majefty, *where too much ; or the* fervice *further provided for by* fupplimental Eftimates, *where the firft has fail'd of anfwering the* real Charge.

III. Thefe Ships (*as faft as repair'd and fitted in their* Hulls) *to be in like manner compleatly fupply'd with fix* Months Sea-Stores, *and thofe feparately laid up and preferv'd for ufe, whenever the Service of their refpective* Ships *fhall call for them.* *To be fur- nifhed with Sea- Stores.*

IV. 'The fame Number of Ships, *and of equal* Rates *with those defign'd by your* Majefty *in your late* Declaration *for* 3000 Men *for the prefent* year, *to be maintain'd at* Sea *in their full* Wages, Victuals, Wear *and* Tear, *for anfwering all your* Foreign Occafions ; *With this* Addition, *that for the advancing* [1] *the* Honour *of your* Majefty *and your* Government, *and the* maintenance *of your* Right *of* Sovereignty *in thefe* Seas, *The prefent Declara- tion for Sea Ser- vice to he madegood and more.*

[1] *advaning corr. S. P.*

Seas, *beyond what appears to have been ever yet provided for it in time of* Peace; *your* Majefty *may* (*inftead of the three* fmall Ships *defign'd by that* Declaration *for your whole* Channel-Guard, *mann'd but with* 275 Men) *have a Squadron of ten* Ships, *confifting of one* 3d. *four* 4th. *three* 5th. *and two* 6th. Rates, *mann'd with no lefs than* [1] 1310 Men, *befides* Yachts.

The prefent want of fmall Frigates to be fupplied by two in each year. V. Laftly, *In confideration of your* Majefty's *prefent and growing* Want *of nimble and lefs chargeable* Frigats, *for anfwering the ordinary* Occafions *of your* Service, *and which* (*through the general* Age *of your* Old *ones*) *you have already in fome degree, and will indifpenfably be yet more conftrain'd to fupply, by* Ships *of lefs* ufe *and greater* Charge; *you may alfo expect a* Recruit *of fuch* Veffels *fupply'd you new off of the* Stocks, *by two in each* year.

A Supplemental 𝔓ropofition, *Relating to your* Ships *at* Sea.

The Ships at Sea to As *to your* Ships *at* Sea, *whofe* Repairs *not being included in the precedent* Propofition,

[1] than *add.* S. P.

fition, *will nevertheless (through their* be repair-
long continuances abroad) require being ed, and
lookt after, as faſt as your Service *will* they and
the whole
admit of their being call'd home; *your* Navy
Majeſty *may reaſonably depend upon ha-* kept for
ving them alſo put into a full Repair, *and* ever ſo,
or new
ſupply'd with ſix Months Sea-Stores, *and* ones [1]
both them, and the whole Fleet, (*when* built, for
once in like manner repair'd) *kept for* 22s. per
Man a
ever ſo (or *made good by* New *ones to be* Month
built in their Rooms, *as they become* Wear and
irrepairable) *without other* Charge *to* Tear.
your Majeſty, *than what ariſes from the*
Allowance *ordinarily made for* Wear
and Tear *during their ſtays abroad, rated
but at* 22 s. per Man *a* Month, *inſtead
of the* 30 s. *at which it has ever hitherto
been eſtimated, and never yet prov'd to
have* Coſt *the* Crown *ſo little.*

Digeſted by the Command, and
ſubmitted with all Humility to
the Correction of Your Majeſty.
S. Pepys.

[1] ones *add.* S. P.

This

The Pro-
pofition
approved.

𝕿𝖍𝖎𝖘 done, and the *King* with the Lord *Treafurer* upon feveral *Debates* approving it; His *Majefty* was pleas'd to determine upon an immediate putting the fame in *Execution,* by fufpending for a time the ordinary Methods of his *Navy,* and calling in to his Affiftance fome other *Hands,* upon whofe *Experience* and *Induftry* (in conjunction with a *felect* Number of the prefent *Board*) he conceived he might with better fecurity rely for the future fuccefs of his *Service: Con-tented* neverthelefs (though[1] from an *Expectation* wholly unfuccefsful) to continue the *Remainder* of them (freed of all other *Services,* than that of bringing-up the *Accounts* of their own time, and more particularly of the *Thirty New Ships*) in the fame full *Salary* during this *Sufpenfion,* which they before enjoy'd, and was not now to be exceeded even to *Thofe* on whom was to lie, the *Care* of *Recovering* in *Three* years, what under them had in the *mifcarrying* coft the Crown *Five.*

Prefent
Methods
of the Na-
vy to be
fufpend-
ed, and
new
hands en-
tertained.

The old
Board
neverthe-
lefs to be
kept in
full Sa-
lary.

[1] though *add.* S. P.   𝕿𝖔=

Towards putting which in prac- *The New* tice, the firſt ſtep was the *Choice* of the *Hands to* Hands ſo to be entertain'd. Wherein *be choſen* (as in the former) His *Majeſty* requiring *Qualifi-* the ſervice of my *Place*, I could not *cations;* think of a more proper *Method* of *and thoſe* diſcharging my *Duty* in it, than by *cations* laying before him (for his better *what.* diſtinguiſhing who *were*, from who *were not* fit for his Uſe, on an Occaſion ſo little able to bear with any miſtake therein) the *Qualifications*, which (as far as they were attainable) I conceiv'd ought to be aim'd at, in preference to all other *Regards*, in this *Election*. And theſe I accordingly with all ſub- miſſion tender'd him, in the Order and Terms following, *Viz.*

I. *A* Practic'd Knowledge *in every* *Practiced* Part of the *Works and* Methods *of your* *Know-* Navy, *both at the* Board *and in your* *ledge.* Yards. *The not diſcerning of which* (*and* *the others that follow*) *appears to have* *coſt your* Royal Brother *and* You *within* *the foremention'd five years, above half a* Million.

II. *A*

Account-
antſhip.

    II. A General Maſtery *in the buſineſs of* Accounts, *though more particularly thoſe incident to the Affairs of* Your Navy.

Vigour.

    III. Vigour of Mind, *joyn'd with approv'd* Induſtry, Zeal, *and* Perſonal *aptneſs for* Labour.

Cloſeneſs
of Appli-
cation.

    IV. An entire Reſignation *of them-ſelves and their whole time to this* Your Service, *without lyableneſs to* Avocation *from other* Buſineſs *or* Pleaſure.

Credit for
integrity
and Loy-
alty.

    V. Laſtly, ſuch Credit *with your* Majeſty *for* Integrity *and* Loyalty, *as may (with the former conditions) lead both* Your Self *and my* Lord Treaſurer, *to an entire confidence of having all done that can be morally expected from them, in the* Advancement *of your* Service, *and the Circumſpect and Orderly* Diſpen-ſing *and* Improving *of your* Treaſure.

The
Kings
choice.

    Which *Limitations* His *Majeſty* having by a deliberate and diſtinct Application of them to the Nature, Importance, and multiplicity of the *ſervices* to be at the ſame time pain-fully and knowingly attended to in

this

this Affair, he judg'd them of behoof
to be obferved; and after a moft
folicitous enquiry made, and Collection had of as many Perfons (and
all, God knows, but few) as the Navy
of *England* could furnifh him with,
qualify'd in any competent wife to anfwer the Characters beforemention'd,
He was pleas'd to fix his choice upon

Sr. *Anthony Deane*.

Sr. *John Berry*.

Mr. *Hewer*.

Mr. *St. Michel*.

And this with fo little privity on
their part to ought of His *Majefties*
Proceedings herein; That could the
King have fatisfy'd himfelf in the
fitnefs of any one other Perfon within
his *Dominions* for fupplying his Room,
Sir *Anthony Dean* had prevail'd for
his being excus'd. So inftant, even
to Offence (as the then Lord *Treafurer*
will, I perfwade my felf, eafily re-
member) were his *Solicitations* to be
fo;

Sir Ant. *Dean's endeavour to avoid it.*

fo ; as having (befides his being now
fettled in a more beneficial *Courfe* of
Negotiation) induftrioufly flung up
(in the Year 1680) the fame *Charge*
of a *Commiffioner* of the *Navy* ; from
his early profpect of its falling into
that *Condition,* in which His *Majefty*
now found it, and out of which he
was therefore pleas'd finally to infift
upon Sir *Anthony Deane's* return to his
Affiftance in the refcuing it.

Nor was the *King* led to this fingu-
larity of Opinion in favour of Sir
Anthony Deane, from any lefs inducement, than what arofe from a
deliberate perufal of a Memorial
I had on that Occafion prepar'd for
him, containing a Lift of every Perfon
then occurring to me (whether in or
out of his *Service*) of more than common reckoning among the *Profeffors*
and *Practicers* of *Shipwrightry* within
this Kingdom. Which Memorial I
here fubjoyn, as evidencing more than
enough the *reafonablenefs* (or rather
neceffity) of this his *Majefty's* Choice,
in

The Kings final in-fifting on his Ser-vice.

And his induce-ment to the Choice of him.

in the bare application of the foremention'd conditions (refpectively) to
the Perfons nam'd therein.

March 9. 168⅚

A 𝕸emorial *for the* King *towards
the* Choice *of a Perfon (qualify'd
as a* Shipwright) *to supply the want
of* Sir Anthony Deane, *in the*
Commiffion *now prepared for the*
Navy ; *the fame feeming Reducible,
To fuch as are in the Service,
either of*

The King, *as his*

	Places.	Perfons.	
Commiffio- ners at the }	*Navy Board* {	*S. J.* Tippets *S. Phin.* Pett	*A Lift of* *the moft* *eminent*
Mafter Ship- wrights at {	*Chatham* *Portfmouth* *Deptford* *Woolwich* *Sheernefs*	Mr. *Lee* Mr. *Betts* Mr. *J. Shifh* Mr. *Lawrence* Mr. *Furzer*	*prefent* *Ship-* *wrights* *of* Eng- land.
Mafter Ship- wrights Af- fiftants at {	*Chatham* { *Portfmouth* *Deptford*	Mr. *Dummer* Mr. *Pett* Mr. *Stiggand* Mr. *Harding*	

Or

Or the Merchants, as

Places.	Perſons.

Private Buil-
ders at
{ *Blackwal* { Sir *H. Johnſon*
{ Mr. *Collins*
Deptford Mr. *R. Caſtle*
Redr. Ratcl. (Mr. *Graves*
&c. in the | Mr. *Jon. Shiſh*
Thames. | Mr. *Barham*
(Mr *Narbrow*

By the King's Command,

S. PEPYS.

The gen-
eral
Scheme of
the Pro-
viſion
now made
of Hands,
for the
ſervice of
the Navy.
And ſo the *Proviſion* made by His *Majeſty* for conducting the *whole* of his *Growing* ſervices, and adjuſting the *Accounts* of thoſe *paſt*, was concerted out of the *Old*, aſſiſted by *New Mem-bers*, under the following *Diſtribution*, Viz.

The

The whole of the Commiſſion.	For the Growing Services.		For adjuſting the paſt Accounts.
	At the Board.	At the Yards.	
Old L. *Falkeland*	L. *Falkeland*		L. *Falkeland*
S. *J. Tippets*			S. *J. Tippets*
S. *R. Haddock.*			S. *R. Haddock*
S. *P. Pett*		S. *P. Pett* at *Chatham*	
S. *J. Narbrough*	S. *J. Narbrough*		
Mr. *Southerne*			Mr. *Southerne*
S. *R. Beach*		S. *R. Beach* at *Portſmouth*	
S. *J. Godwin*	S. *J. Godwin*		
New S. *Ant. Deane*	S. *A. Dean*		
S. *J. Berry*	S. *J. Berry*		
Mr. *Hewer*	Mr. *Hewer.*		
Mr. S. *Michael*		Mr. St. *Michel* at *Dept.* & *Woolw.*	

The Lord *Falkeland* remaining
Treaſurer for the Whole.

𝕻𝖚𝖗𝖘𝖚𝖆𝖓𝖙 to this *Scheme,* the *King* by his *Letters Patents* of the 17*th.* of *April* 1686. after declaring that the *Enquiries* he had made ſince his coming to the *Throne* into the *State* of his *Royal Navy,* had diſcover'd it ſuch, as

The Kings Commiſſion purſuant thereto. April 17. 1686.

as call'd for some extraordinary *Appli-*
cation for the putting it into that
Condition of *Force* and *Discipline,*whereto
his *Royal* Purpose was to restore and
advance it ; and that the weight

and diversity of *Works* to be now
perform'd, with greater *Vigour* and
Good-Husbandry than he found to have
been for some time [1] exercis'd therein,
requir'd a *Distribution* of them answer-
able to the different *Qualifications* of
the *Persons* he had to intrust with
them ; constituted these *Gentlemen* his
Commissioners, charg'd with the *Duties*
assign'd to each in the foregoing *Table,*
and the *Instructions* annext to their
Commission. Among which, to those
intrusted with the *growing services,* this
was one, *Viz.*

    That forasmuch as from the present
Disorders under which the whole business
of the Office *of his* Navy *was fallen,*
through the liberty *for some time taken*
of committing the most important Parts
of it to Clerks *and inferiour* Instru-
ments, *in lieu of the* Officers *themselves*

---
[1] sometime *corr.* S. P.
                                              per-

perfonally charg'd therewith, He had (anfwerable to what was fuccefsfully done by His Royal Grand-father, *King* James, *on a like Occafion) thought it neceffary to put the fame into* Commiffion, *until the ancient* Order *and* Difcipline *of it being recover'd, he might with fafety reftore it to its former* Method *of* Infti-tution; *He declares His Royal* Intention *and* Expectation *to be, that thefe his* Commiffioners *hold themfelves* jointly accountable *for the well performance of the* whole, *and ftand* equally *charge-able with the* Failures *found therein.*

𝕬𝖓𝖉 fo they enter'd upon the *Execution* of this *Commiffion,* as from *Lady-Day* 1686; directing their firft ftep to the finding out the true Source of this *fo unexampled Evil* they were now to contend with, in the moft tender Part of their Charge, namely, the *New Ships.* Than which as noth-ing could be more deferving their niceft fearch, with regard to the pub-lick import of the fubject of it. So neither could any thing be of more

The Com-miffion to operate from Lady Day. 1686. *Enquiry into the true Caufe of the* New Ships *decays.*

particular moment to them, whom
the King had thus intrufted with the
Cure, than an explicite Knowledge of
the *Origine* of the *Difeafe*.

Taking therefore this for the proper
place of doing it, I here infert a fhort
Account of the iffue of thofe *enquiries*
of thefe Gentlemen thereinto; and
the rather, for the fake of the *unac-*
Vulgar *countablenefs* of their *Suggeftions*, who
fuggefti- would have it wholly imputable to
ons touch- the *Haftinefs* of the *Building*, the
ing the *Greennefs* of the *Stuff*, and efpecial
fame. *Effects* of the *Eaft-Country-Timber* and
Plank wrought thereon.

Haftinefs To the two former of which, it
in Build- was made appear to His *Majefty*, that
ing and the *Ship* the *quickeft* built of the whole
Green- number lay full *nine* months upon the
nefs of Stocks, and but *feven* of the thirty lefs
Stuff, not than an entire *Year*. Whereas diverfe
charge- Inftances were produc'd out of his
able *Old Navy*, where the *Timber* had been
there- ftanding, cut, and converted, and the
with. *Ships* built therewith, and launched
in *fix months*; without having one
Plank

Plank fhifted in them (but for *Shot*) in *Eight* or *Nine Years* after. While on the contrary, *three* and *twenty* of thefe *Thirty* lay from *one* to full *two*, *three*, and *four Years* in building, and the laft of them more than *five*; till above *one hundred pounds* was demanded by her *Builder* for repairing the Decays of her very *Keel*, as fhe lay upon the *Stocks*.

And for what concerns the Ufe of *Eaft-Country-Stuff*; it was no lefs alfo fhewn to the *King*, that feveral *Ships* were then fubfifting in his *Navy*, planked with no other, which after the fame Service of *eight* or *nine Years*, were by many degrees in better *Condition*, than moft of thefe at *three*. *Nor the ufe of Eaft-Country-Stuff.*

It was moreover obferv'd, that not above *Five* hundred of *Five* and *Thirty Thoufand* Loads of *Timber*, provided for thefe Ships, were of *Eaft-Country-Growth*. *Forreign Timber little.*

And that for *Plank*; had the *Officers* of the *Navy* (after twenty years currant ufe of it) met with any prefent Ground *Forreign Plank, not wanting, in this particular case.*

Their Materials, (as well Forreign as Domestick,) well reported of by the Master-Builders.

Universal Practice in approval of East-Country-Stuff.

No Ships worse, than some that had none of that Commodity in them.

for fufpecting it, there had been *English* enough (and of proper *Thickneffes*) contracted and paid for by the *King*, for anfwering all the Occafions of their *Buttocks* and *Hoodings* from the *Water's Edge* to their *Gun-deck-Ports* (where this *Evil* was obferv'd principally to feize them) without reforting to the ufe of one Inch of *Eaft-Country.*

The *Mafter-Builders* too, unanimoufly afferted the good Condition of all the *Timber* and *Plank* (whether *English* or *Forreign*) us'd on this Work, equal to the beft they had ever known in the *Navy:* Befides the univerfality of the Practice of all the *Northern Nations,* and not them only, but the *Dutch, French,* and (for feveral years paft) our *own Merchant Builders* too, in the ufe of this *Commodity.* Nor (in a word) did any one Ship appear, among the whole *Thirty,* more complaining, than fome of them, upon which not one Foot of *Eaftland-Plank* or *Timber* had been wrought.

All

All which notwithſtanding; ſuch *Import-* did theſe *Gentlemen* eſteem the Weight *ance of* of this *Cauſe*, with reſpect no leſs to *a right* the *fatality* on one hand attending *determin-* the uſe of this *Commodity* upon theſe *ation in* Ships, in caſe the ſame ſhould be *this mat-* found truely *faulty*; than on the *ter.* other, to the conſequences of the *Miſtake*, ſhould it indeed prove other- wiſe, at a ſeaſon, wherein the *ſervice* of it was become next to indiſpenſable, for the preſent Repair of the *Fleet*; That their *Commiſſion* was no ſooner opened, but a ſolemn *Conference* was *A ſolemn* held by them with all the Eminent *Confer-* *Maſter Builders* in the River of *Thames*, *ence with* upon this *Subject*. The *Iſſue* of which *the moſt* *eminent* having been preſented to the *King*, *Mr. Ship-* he was pleas'd to make it ſo much *wrights* a matter of *State*, as to command my *of Eng-* bringing it ſome time after to the *land* *about it.* *Council-Table*. Of whoſe *Reſolution* thereon, and the reſult of the fore- going *Conference*, I have ſubjoyn'd Copies, as of a *Matter* moſt worthy the Notice of every *Engliſh Gentleman*, tho

tho more particularly thofe, who are converfant in the *Timber-Trade* of this Kingdom.

RESOLUTIONS,

Taken at a Conference *held at the* Office *of the* Navy, *April.* 17. 1686. *between His Majefty's* Commiffioners *there, and us the under-written* Ship-wrights, *upon* Enquiries *then propos'd by the* Secretary *of the* Admiralty *on behalf of His* Majefty, *touching the prefent* Condition *of this* Kingdom, *in reference to* 𝔓lank *for Ship-Building.*

Enquiry I.

How far it may be depended on, that England *may at this day fupply it felf with a fufficiency of that* Commodity, *for anfwering the Occafions both of the* Merchants *and His* Majefty's *fervice* (*in the State the* Royal Navy *thereof now is*) *without* Foreign *Help?*

Refo-

Refolution.

That it is in no wife to be rely'd *Plank not* on. Forafmuch as from the want *fufficient of Englifh* of *Plank* of our *own Growth*, and *growth to* confequently the highnefs of *Price anfwer* of what we have ; the *Shipwrights* of *all the* this Kingdom (even in our *Out-Ports*, *prefent occafions* as well as in the River of *Thames) for the* have been for many years paft, driven *fame.* to refort to fupplys *from Abroad*[1], and are fo at this day, to the Occafioning their fpending of *One Hundred* Loads of *Forreign*, for every *Twenty* of *Englifh*. Befides, were our *own* Stock more ; the exclufion of *Forreign* Goods would foon render the Charge of Building *infupportable*, by raifing the *Price* of the Commodity to double what it is, and more, at the pleafure of the *Seller*.

Enquiry II.

From whence is the beft Forreign Plank *underftood to be brought?*

[1] *Aboard corr.* S. P.

Refo-

Resolution.

Best for-
reign
Plank
from
whence.

Either out of the *East-Sea* from *Dantzick, Quinborow,* or *Riga* of the Growth of *Poland* and *Prussia,* or from *Hambrough,* namely, that fort thereof, which is Shipt from thence of the Growth of *Bohemia,* diftinguifhed by its Colour, as being much more black than the other, and rendred fo (as is faid) by its long fobbing in the water, during its Paffage thither.

Enquiry III.

What Proportion *this* Forrein Plank *may be reckoned to bear to the* Englifh, *with regard to its* Ufe, Coft, *and* Durablenefs?

Resolution.

The Ufe,
Coft, and
Durable-
ness of
forreign
Plank
compared
with
Englifh.

For fo much as concerns *fmaller Veffels* of Fourfcore Tuns downwards (whofe works call not for more than 2 Inch Plank, of 20 Foot long at the higheft, meeting at 13 and 14 Inches in breadth) our *Englifh* Plank will
(from

(from the Nature of the Wood) laſt
longer than any *Forreign* of the ſame
Dimenſions. But for *Ships* of 300
Tuns upwards, which require the ſervice of 3 and 4 Inch-Plank from 26
to 40 Foot long, meeting at 14 or
15 Inches breadth at the Top-end;
Univerſal practice ſhews, that the
White Crown-*Plank* of *Pruſſia*, and
the fore-mentioned *Black* of *Bohemia*,
do in their durableneſs equal or
rather exceed that of Our *Engliſh*
Production of like Dimenſions.

Which we conceive to ariſe from
this plain Reaſon, *viz.* That the
Forreign Oak being of much quicker
growth than ours, their Trees arrive
at a Stature capable of yielding *Plank*
of theſe *Meaſures*, while they are yet
in their ſound and vigorous *State* of
growing; whereas that of *England*
advancing in its Growth more ſlowly,
arrives not at theſe Dimenſions, till
it be come to or rather is paſt the
full of its *Strength*; fifty *Years* ſufficing
for raiſing the *Forreign*, to what the

*Conject-
ure at the
Phyſical
reaſon of
the differ-
ent dura-
bleneſs
of for-
reign and
Engliſh
Plank of
the larger
Dimen-
ſions.*

Eng-

Englifh will not be brought in an hundred and fifty.

But whether we are right or not in this Reafoning, it is upon daily experience moft evident; that our *Eaft-India*, and other *Ships* of greateft *Burthen*, built with this large *Forreign* Plank, well chofen, prove in their *Durablenefs* without exception; variety of Inftances lying before us, of *Ships* built wholy with *Englifh* ftuff, (as well in His *Majefties* Yards as *Merchants*) which have perifh'd in half the time, others of like Burthen, compos'd wholly of *Forreign*, have been obferv'd to do.

From hence alfo it is, that though *Englifh Plank* of *Short* Lengths, cut out of young *Growing* Timber, is manifeftly better than *Eaft-Country*, and therefore is preferred thereto in laying of a *Gun-Deck*, as far as the three ftreaks next the Ships fides, where fhort ftuff will ferve (the *Quality* of its *Wood* bearing better with being kept *Wet* and *Dry*, as it generally is

in

in that place. Yet where (upon the fame *Gun-deck*) *long Plank* is neceffary, that of *Forreign* growth is for Strength and duration always preferr'd, from the reafon (as we conceive) before given, namely, of its being cut while in its *Vigour*, which the *Englifh* will not admit, fo as to bear thofe *Scantlings*.

And to this is to be further added, the general *Waninefs*, want of *Breadth* at the *Top-end*, and ill method of *Converfion* of our *Englifh* Plank; daily practice fhewing, that twenty Loads of *Forreign* fhall in working go further upon a Ships fide or Deck, than a hundred *Loads* of like Lengths of *Englifh*, after its *Wanes* and other *Defects* fhall be cut away. *General waninefs, want of Breadth at the Top end, and ill Converfion of Englifh Plank.*

Moreover it is yet to be noted, that in planking of a Ship with *Forreign* Plank, the Builder fhall not be driven to put in above three or four Pieces, where in a like Ship done with *Englifh*, he fhall be obliged to ufe a hundred; to the no lefs impairment of the *ftrength* of the Work, than *Encreafe of Work and Charge arifing therefrom.*

than increafe of its *Charge*, both in Stuff and Labour.

So that upon the whole, our unanimous *Opinion* is; that large *Plank*, well chofen, of the *Forreign* growths beforemention'd, is in its fervice at leaft as *durable*, in its coft lefs *Chargeable*, and the ufe of it (through the fcarcity of *Englifh*) become at this day *indifpenfable*.

Jonas Shifh.	*Hen. Johnfon.*
Pet. Norberry.	*Abra. Greaves.*
Jof. Lawrence.	*John Shifh.*
Ja. Yeames.	*Wil. Collins.*
	Rob. Caftel.

By *the* Commiffioners *of the* NAVY.

We do fully concur in the *Refolutions* above-written.

A. Deane.
J. Narbrough.
J. Berry.
Ph. Pet.
Wil. Hewer.
B. S. Michel.

Mem=

Memorandum, That thefe *Refolu-* *Prefenta-* *tions* from the Body of the *Mafter* *tion* *thereof* Builders of *England,* confirm'd by the *to the* *Commiffioners* of the *Navy,* to my King and Enquiries touching *Foreign* Plank, *from him* were Communicated by me to His *to the* *Council-* *Majefty* (my Lord *Treufurer* prefent) *Board.* *October* the *7th.* and by His fpecial Command prefented to Him again (with a Memorial attending it) at the *Council Table,* Oct. 8*th.* 1686.

S. PEPYS.

At the Court *at* Whitehall
Oct. 8. 1686.

PRESENT

The *Kings* moft Excellent *Majefty.*

His R. H. Pr. *George* of *Denmark,* &c.

A Paper *having been this day* (*by his* Order of Majefties *command*) *prefented to the* Council Board *by Mr.* Pepys *Secretary of the* *in appro-* Admiralty *of* England, *containing cer-* *confirma-* *tain* Refolutions *taken at a* Conference *tion of* *held at the Office of the Navy the* 17. *of* *the fore-* *going* April *Report.*

April *laft, between his Majefties* Commiffioners *there, and the Body of the
moft eminent* Ship - Builders *of this
Kingdom, upon* Enquiries *propofed to
them by the faid* Secretary *on behalf and
by direction of his* Majefty, *touching
the prefent condition of* England *in
reference to* Plank *for Ship-building,
and the faid* Paper *being now read and
folemnly confider'd;* His Majefty *was
pleafed to declare his being fo far convinc'd there-from of the* fafety, benefit,
and prefent neceffity *of making ufe of*
Plank *of* Foreign *growth in the Building
and Repairing of His* Royal Navy, *as
to refolve; That the* Principal Officers
and Commiffioners *of his* Navy *be at
liberty to contract for and make ufe in
his Services aforefaid of* Oaken Plank
of Foreign *growth, of the Sorts mention'd
in the* Refolution *to the Second Enquiry
contain'd in the faid* Paper; *and to
Order, that the faid* Original Paper
under the Hands of the Commiffioners
of the Navy *and* Mafter Builders, *be
(for the* publick Importance *thereof)*
care-

carefully laid up and preferv'd among the
Papers and Records of the Council-Table.

John Nicholas.

The prefent *Effects* of which laft *The true*
Papers and the *Obfervations* next pre- *Grounds*
ceding, amounting to nothing lefs *of the*
New-
than a plain *Detection* of the *Vanity* *Ships De-*
of thofe *fuggeftions* touching the Root *cays.*
of this *Calamity*; Nought remain'd
whereon the fame could with any
appearance of *Confequence* be charg'd,
fave the plain *Omiffion* of the neceffary
and ordinary *Cautions* us'd for the
preferving of *New-built Ships.* Divers *Want of*
of them appearing not to have been *Graving*
once *Grav'd* nor brought into *Dock,* *& bring-*
ing into
fince they were Launched. Others *Dock.*
that had been *Dockt,* fent out again
in a *Condition* needing to be brought-
in a fecond time. Their *Holds* not *Holds not*
clean'd nor air'd, but (for want of *clean'd*
nor ayr'd.
Gratings and opening their *Hatches* *Gratings*
and *Scuttles*) fuffer'd to heat and *wanting.*
moulder, till I have with my own *Hatches*
and Scut-
Hands gather'd *Toad-ftools* growing *tles not*
in *opened.*

Not heel'd or breemed.

Expofed to the Sun, with their Sides un-watered.

Not Bal-lafted enough to deepen them in the Water.

Ports not opened in dry wea-ther.

Scuppers wanting on the Gun-decks, in wet.

Planks not open-ed upon the firft difcovery

in the moft confiderable of them, as big as my *Fifts.* Some not once *heel'd* or *breem'd* fince their building, but expos'd in hot weather to the *Sun,* broiling in their *Buttocks* and elfe-where, for want of cooling with *Water* (according to the Practice of our own, as well as all *Forreign* Nations) and that *Expofure* yet magnifi'd, by their want of *Ballaft* for bringing them deep enough into the *Water.* *Port-Ropes* alfo wanting wherewith to open the *Ports,* for airing them in *Dry* weather ; and *Scuppers* upon their *Gun-decks* in *Wet,* to prevent the fink-ing of *Rain* through their fhrunken *Seams* into their *Holds* and among their *Timbers. Planks* not open'd upon the firft Difcovery of their *Decays,* nor *Pieces* put in, where defective ; but inftead thereof, repair'd only with *Caps* of *Board*[1] and *Canvas.* Which ought alfo to have been done upon the *Ordinary Eftimate* of the *Navy,* that provides for every thing needful to the *Prefervation* of Ships in *Harbour,*

[1] Boards corr. S. P.

but

but more efpecially for the Graving *of their*
one *Third* of the whole every *Year*; *Decays,*
whereas fome (even of the *Old Ships*) *nor thofe*
appear not to have been fo look'd *Decays*
after, in five or fix. *duely looked to.*

From which, and other like *Omif-* *The effect*
fions, it could not but fall out (as *of thefe*
indeed it did) that fome of thefe un- *Omiffions*
fortunate *Ships* were already become *obferv'd.*
rotten, while others built of the very
fame Stuff, at the *fame Place*, by the
fame Hand, and within the very *fame*
Time for *Merchant-fervice*, fuc⟨c⟩eeded
well and continu'd fo.

𝔄nd with the *Navy* thus diforder'd, *The En-*
thefe *Gentlemen* (as I have faid) enter'd *try and*
upon their *Commiffion*. And with what *¹procedure*
Spirit and under what View they pro- *of ¹ thefe*
ceeded thereon, will be beft Collected *Commif-*
from their own *Annual Reports* thereof *fioners.*
to the *King*, confonant (through the
whole) to the few following Para-
graphs, *viz.*

𝔄uguft 1687.

We tender in all humility to Your
Ma-

Majefty *our humble* Reprefentation *of the* Effeds *of that* Commiffion, *to which you were pleas'd to call us; and which we have endeavour'd to performe with a fincerity and plainnefs, anfwerable (as far as we are able) to the extraordinarinefs of that Favour, wherewith (without our* expedation) *we were called thereto*——————

With Sincerity and plainnefs.

Called by the King without their expedation.

Whereas among other the Works of your Navy, *that of* Graving *and well performing the* Ordinary *Repairs of your Ships in* Harbour, *holds a principal Place. As that, to the want of which, a great (if not the greateft) fhare of the* Calamity *whereinto they (and particular⟨l⟩y the* Thirty New Ones) *have been fuffer'd to fall, is moft rightfully to be imputed; and has therefore the firft place given* ¹ *it by your* Majefty *in this* propofition. *We have moft diligently apply'd our felves to an effedual anfwering every* part *thereof (both as to* Works *and* payments) *as far at leaft as the* Defeds *of the faid Ships, fo long in* Arrear, *could within this time be difcover'd and purfu'd*——————

Graving and ordinary Repairs.

The Decays long in arrear.

¹ giving; *corr.* S. P.

When

When it shall be consider'd, how deeply *the Ships were infected with that evil, by which they were (even in their* Thick- est stuff*) become* rotten *and reduc'd to* powder. *It seems a matter of too great presumption (without wholly strip- ping them) to* undertake *against any pos- sible* remains or returns *of the said* evil. *But this we take Liberty to say*———

And however more or less successful our Managements *may be found to be in the well husbanding of your* Treasure *herein; We are not conscious of being* able to mend it, were we to Act the same over again, and the Gain or Loss arising therefrom to affect our own Purses, as they now do Your Majesty's.*

And their in- fection too deep, for any un- dertaking of their cure with- out whol- ly striping them.

Good Hus- bandry herein af- serted.

Falkeland.   J. Godwin.
A. Deane.   Ph. Pett.
J. Narbrough.   W. Hewer.
J. Berry.   B. St. Michel.

August 1688.

Though we need no greater Assurance, *than what Your Majesty has already on every Occasion given us, of Your Gracious*

Opinion

Opinion of our Humble Endeavours *in this Your Service. Yet cannot we forbear*

The effects of their Service greater, had not the Works proved worse than estimated.

observing to Your Majesty, that the Effects *thereof might have prov'd greater (though our* Industry *could not) had not the State of Your* Ships *prov'd much worse, and by consequence the* Work *and* Charge *of them weightier, than they were Estimated in the Surveys and Calculations, upon which that* Proposition *was founded, and the Execution of it committed to us; besides the difficulties we have had to*

Obstructions industriously offered them and whence.

contend with, from Obstructions *and* Hardships *industriously put upon us (both from* Sea *and* Shore*) by those to whom our Methods of* Good Husbandry *and* Dispatch *proved less grateful, than the* Laxeness *in both, to which they had for some time been accustom'd———*

The well performance of the Works.

As to the complete Performance *of these* Works, *as far as Matters of this kind can be judg'd of, and in a Case so extraordinary as that of the* State *whereinto Your Royal* Navy *was fallen at the time of your calling us to the remedying it; We have not only our own* Observations,

tions, *and the amplenefs of thofe our* Orders *by which the faid* Works *were directed to be performed; but the* Reports *of your* Mafter-Builders *charg'd with the conducting them, confirm'd by your* Commiffioners *of the* Yards *where they were feverally perform'd. Beyond which we cannot conceive any thing capable of being added towards the fatisfying either* Your Majefty, *or our felves therein. And though we do not believe fo much to have been ever before fhewn in the Cafe of a like* Fleet. *Yet, regard being had to what* Experience *dayly informs us, of the* Defects *difcover'd upon ranfacking of their* Seams *by the* Caulkers, *we dare not miflead your* Majefty *to think, that (after fo general and deep a* Decay, *as this* Fleet *was fallen into, before any fitting* Application *was made for its* Remedy) *all the* Care *that has been taken in the fhifting of its* Timbers *and* Plank (*as far as any* Defects *have appear'd*) *can upon frefh* Ranfacking, *fecure your* Majefty *againft the appearance of further* Remains, *till the firft* Materials *about*

Evidenced by their own Obfervations. The amplenefs of their Orders. The Reports of the Mr. Builders, and Yard Commiffioners. And yet not to be relyed on againft the poffible Returns or Remains of this Evil.

about the Breadths *and adjacent* Parts
(*efpecially of the* New Ships) *fhall by
degrees be entirely remov'd*————

The Ships yet to be finifhed for compleating the Propofition. It refts to give Your Majefty the Names of your Ships under prefent Repair, and thofe remaining to be repair'd when they fhall be finifh'd for compleating your whole Navy, according to Mr. Pepys's Propofition, Viz.

Ships under Repair.		Remaining to be Repair'd.	
Ships,	Yard.	Ships,	Yard.
St. *Michael* Roy. *Kathe-rine*	} Chath.	*Prince Victory Royal Oak*	} Chath.
Brittannia St. *George Monck*	} Portfm.	*King-Fi-fher*	} Deptf.
Happy Re-turn Oxford	} Woolw.		
Portland Phænix	} Deptf.		

Falkeland.   Ph. Pett.
A. Deane.   W. Booth.
J. Berry.   W. Hewer.
B. S. Michel.

This

This while in doing, towards the
Amendment of matters on *Shore*, and
the *State* of the *Ships* in *Harbour*; no
lefs thoughtfulnefs was at work for
the *Recovery* of good *Difcipline* and
Reformation of *Diforders* a. *Sea.* And
this purfu'd, to the drawing a no
inconfiderable *Encreafe* of ftanding
Charge upon the *Crown*, the more furely
to effect his Majefties defires herein,
with the *fatisfaction* of his *Commanders*
and other his *Officers* and *Seamen* inter-
efted in the fame. The evidencing
of which will not need more than
one of fundry inftances to be produc'd
of it, namely, that of the *Eftablifhment*
in *July* 1686. (of near *Date* with the
foregoing *Commiffion*) the Tenor whereof follows.

*His Majefties Regulation in the bufinefs
of* Plate-Carriage, &c. *with his Eftablifhment of an Allowance to his* Sea-
Commanders *for their* Tables *and
other* Encouragements *to them, their
Officers, and Companies.*

James

*Difcipline
to be re-
covered
and Dif-
orders re-
formed at
Sea.*

*And not
without
charge
to the
Crown,
for the
better
fatisfac-
tion of
Comman-
ders, &c.*

*Inftanced
in the
Eftablifh-
ment
about
Captains
Tables,
Forreign
Prizes,
&c.*

James R.

'WHereas from the *Enquiries* by us folemnly made (fince our acceffion to the *Throne* of this our Kingdom of *England*) into the [1] *State* of our *Royal Navy*, and the general *Diforders* Diforders into which both it and its *in the* Difcipline have of late years fallen, *Navy en-* we are (among the many other *Evils* *quired* *into, by* difcovered therein, and which we *the King.* have already in great meafure provided *Remedies* to) arrived at a full Information in that particular one, whereto our Service is in a moft efpecial manner expofed, from the liberty taken by *Commanders* of our *Ships* (upon all opportunities of private profit) of converting the Service *Particu-* of our faid Ships to their own ufe, *larly the* and the total neglect of the *Publick* *diverting* Ends for which they, at our great *the pub-* *lick fer-* Charge, are fet forth and maintained, *vice of* namely, the annoying of our *Enemies,* *his Ships* the protecting the Eftates of our *to private* Trading-Subjects, and the fupport of *ufes.* our

[1] the *repeated in ed.*; *corr.* S. P.

our honour with *Forreign Princes*. And forafmuch alfo as this *Evil* feems principally to arife from the univerfal abufe of the liberty for fome time indulged to Our faid *Commanders*, of Tranfporting of *Plate*, *Bullion*, and *Jewels*; to the occafioning thereby the faid General mif-employment of our *Ships*, and our want of thofe full and frequent *Accounts* of the *Proceedings* of our Commanders abroad, which by their known *Inftructions* they ftand obliged to give us. Our *Will* and *pleafure* is, and it is hereby folemnly declared. *Arifing from the abufed liberty of carrying Plate, &c.*

' I. That no *Admiral*, *Commander in Chief*, *Captain* of any of our *Ships*, or other *Officers* ferving us therein, fhall prefume from henceforward upon any pretence, or by vertue of any former Allowance, Inftruction, or Practice whatfoever, to receive direct, or permit to be received, on board any of our faid Ships, any *Mony*, *Plate*, *Bullion*, *Jewels*, or other *Merchandize* or *Goods* (fine or grofs) whatfoever, whether *Plate carriage, &c. reftrained.*
be-

belonging to Strangers or our own
Subjects, either under pretext of con-
cealing or protecting the fame, or
the Tranfporting thereof from Port
to Port, or from any Forreign Port
for *England*, whether upon *Application*
to them made by any our *Merchant-
Subjects* in Forreign parts, or from
any other inducement whatfoever,
faving by Written Warrant under
our own *Royal* hand, and that only;
upon pain of being (on conviction)
immediately difcharged from their
prefent, and rendred incapable of
any future Employment in our Service; as alfo of refunding to the
ufe of our *maimed* Seamen of the
Cheft at *Chatham*, the full value of
the profits they fhall be found to
have made by any violation of this
our Order, and of fuffering fuch further punifhment, as by the *Laws* of
the *Sea*, they fhall become liable to
for the fame.

‘ II. That none of our aforefaid
General Officers or private *Commanders*
fhall

fhall, (upon like forfeiture and pen- *The like*
alties) prefume to carry, or direct *as to*
the carrying any *Paffenger* or *Paf-* *carrying*
fengers (whether ftrangers or others) *of Paf-*
of what Degree or Quality foever, *fengers.*
from one place to another, in any
of our *Ships* of *War* under their
Command, unlefs by like particular
Order given in Writing from our
felf for their fo doing; fuch only
excepted, as by the Eleventh Article *With Ex-*
of our prefent General *InftruXions* *ceptions.*
they are obliged to receive and give
paffage to; namely, our *SubjeXs*
redeemed from *Slavery*, *Shipwreckt*,
or taken at Sea out of *Forreign*
Ships.

'III. That all *Admirals* and *Com-* *Copies of*
manders in Chief of Our Ships do for *all Sail-*
the time to come take care, that as *ing Or*
often as they fhall have occafion of *dersiffued*
giving *Orders* for the proceeding of *or receiv-*
any of Our *Ships* under their Com- *ed at Sea*
mand on any Service, the fame be *tranfmit-*
done in Writing under their hands, *ted to the*
with *Copies* thereof to be fent by the *Secretary*
firft *Admir-*
alty.

firſt opportunities of conveyance (by Land and Sea) to the *Secretary* of our *Admiralty* for our information. And that the fame be in like manner done by the *Commanders* of every of our *private* Ships, in Tranſmitting to our faid *Secretary* for our like Information, *Copies* of every *Order* they ſhall receive from their Admiral, Commander in chief, or other Superiour Officer.

The like as to Advices of the Kings Ships coming into forreign Ports, and Abſtracts of their Journals.

'IV. That every of our fore-mentioned *Officers* and *Commanders* reſpectively, do obſerve, that as often as our Service requires their going into any *Forreign Port*, they do by the firſt *Poſt* after their arrival, (and ſo from *Poſt* to *Poſt* during their ſtay there) give us (through the hand of our ſaid *Secretary*) a particular Account of their *Proceedings*, from the date of their laſt, with *Abſtracts* of their *Journals* during that time; and that care be taken for their leaving the like with our *Conſul* or other publick *Miniſter* in that Place, to be by him for-

forwarded to our faid *Secretary*, by
the firft Conveyance after their de-
parture thence; fo as we may at all
times have a conftant and thorough
knowledge of the *Condition, Services*,
and *Proceedings* of all and every of
our *Ships* employed on Forreign Service, with the occafions of the fame.

Laftly, That at the end of each *The like*
Voyage, an entire *Book* containing *at the*
end of the
a perfect *Journal* thereof, together *Voyage*,
with a *Book* of *Entries* to be kept of *as to their*
all *Orders*, either iffued or received *Journals*,
(as before) by them therein, be de- *and En-*
try-Books
livered for our ufe to our faid *Secre- of Orders*.
tary* of the *Admiralty* (and fworn to
if required) by every of our faid
Admirals, Commanders in *Chief*, and
private *Commanders*, immediately upon
their coming into Port to be laid up,
and before the paying off of the
Ships whereto they refpectively be-
long. Both which *Books* our faid
Secretary is to caufe to be well ex-
amined by himfelf, or fuch other
Perfon as fhall be exprefly appointed
thereto,

thereto, in order to a *Report* to be therefrom made to us, of the different Degrees of *care* or *neglect* wherewith thefe and all other our *Orders* fhall appear to have been obferved, and our receiving full fatisfaction from them therein, before the payment of their *Wages*, or the further *Allowance* hereafter appointed in confideration of their good Service during their faid *Voyage*.

Univer-
fal Ob-
fervation
of thefe
Rules in-
joyn'd.

'Of all which as well every our faid *Admirals, Commanders* in *Chief*, private *Commanders* of our *Ships*, and other the Officers within mentioned, as our prefent *Secretary* of our *Admiralty*, and the *Secretary* of our *Admiralty* for the time being, are hereby required to yield full and conftant obedience and conformity, as they will anfwer the contrary at their perils.

And en-
couraged
by the
Eftablifh-
ment of
an extra-

𝕬𝖓𝖉 to the end, that with the Provifion thus made towards the recovery and advancement of the *Honour, Difcipline*, and *Profperity* of our *Naval-*
Service,

Service, We may at the fame time *ordinary*
Teftifie our like *Royal* Inclination to *allow-*
the giving all reafonable *Encourage-* *ance to*
ment to thofe, who fhall from hence- *manders*
forward be employed as *Commanders* *for fup-*
in any of our *Ships*; thereby as well *port of*
to excite and oblige them to a ftrict *Tables.*
complyance with thefe and all other
our *Royal* Refolutions and Orders, as
the better to enable them to fupport
the *Charge* and *Dignity* of their faid
Employments and *Entertainment* therein,
without reforting to *Methods* of doing
it fo injurious to our *Honour* and
Service, and wafteful of our *Treafure*,
as thofe before-mentioned have been.

'We are in the firft place gracioufly
pleafed (in favour to our faid *Com-*
manders) to take upon our felf an
encreafe of *Charge*, beyond what has
ever hitherto been at any one time
done by any of our *Royal* Predeceffors,
namely, by granting (as we hereby
do) to the *Commanders* of every of
our *Ships* and *Veffels* (*Yachts* only ex-
cepted) an annual *Allowance* (over and
above

above the value of the *Victualling* they now enjoy in common with their Ship's Companies) for the fupport of their *Tables,* proportioned to the refpective Rates of the Ships and Veffels they fhall happen feverally to Command.

This Al-lowance to begin, when. The faid *Allowance* to commence upon thofe of our Ships which are now fitting forth, and fhall at any time hereafter be fitted forth to the *Seas,* from the Date and Delivery of their Commanders and Signing Officers joynt *Certificates* to the *Secretary* of our *Admiralty,* and *Commiffioners* of our Navy, of their Ships being compleatly fitted for the Sea, and in readinefs to Execute our final Orders for their Sailing. And upon fuch of our *Ships* as are at this prefent abroad; from the day of their Commanders receiving from our faid *Secretary* (which he is with all convenient fpeed to difpatch to them) Copies of this our Order; and to be continued both on the one and the other to the Determination of their refpective *Voyages.*

‘ The

' The value of which allowance hereby fo granted is as follows.

A Table of the Annual Allowance of a Sea-Commander of each Rate.			
Rate	Prefent Wages.	Prefent Victualling.	Additional Grant for his Table.
	£ s. d.	£ s. d.	£ s d.
1	273 15 0	12 3 4	250 0 0
2	219 00 0	12 3 4	200 0 0
3	182 00 0	12 3 4	166 5 0
4	136 10 0	12 3 4	124 5 0
5	109 10 0	12 3 4	100 0 0
6	91 00 0	12 3 4	83 0 0

The value of that allowance.

'Wherein our *Royal Intention* is, that this *allowance* for *Tables* granted to our faid *Commanders* as Captains of Private Ships, fhall not be conftrued to the taking away or diminifhing ought of what has been heretofore Eftablifhed to *Flag-Officers*, upon Account of their *Flags*.

Without leffening the allowance already eftablifhed to Flags.[1]

'And that we may yet the more effectually excite to a vigorous profe-

[1] *Flags*] *Fags* in ed. corr. S. P.

cution

A further Grant, to them, their Officers, and Companies, of the whole value of the Prizes taken from the People of Barbary. cution of our *Service*, such of our said *Commanders* as shall be by us employed in our Wars with any of the people of *Barbary*, (such as that wherein we now are, and have, to the great Expence of our *Treasure* and hazard to our *Subjects* Trading into those Seas, for several years been engaged with those of *Sally*) we are graciously pleas'd farther to grant to such our *Commanders*, the full benefit of all Prizes, (both *Hulls*, *Furniture*, *Lading* and *Slaves*) that shall be by them taken, whether of *Ships* of *War*, or *Merchant Men*; saving only the Vessels of our *Subjects* happening to have fallen into the hands of such our *Enemies*. In which case, the *Salvage* only of the Vessels of our Subjects so rescued, shall go to the *Retakers*.

'The whole of which forementioned *Prizes* and *Salvage* shall be divided between the *Commander* or *Commanders*, of such our Ship or Ships (with their *Officers* and *Companies*) as were concerned

cerned in the Chafe and *Capture* of the faid Prizes, according to the *Law* and *practice* of the *Sea*.

'Provided always, that no part of the *Charge* of fecuring or maintaining any of the Veffels, Lading, or Companies of the faid *Prizes*, fhall be placed to our Account, from the day wherein the fame fhall be firft brought into any *Chriftian* Port; and that the faid *Prizes* be carried into Port, with as little Charge as may be to us, and without any interruption to the *fervice* wherein our faid Ships were imployed at the time of the *Capture*. *Conditions of this Allowance.*

'Laftly, we are hereby gracioufly pleafed further to declare to all our faid *Admirals, Commanders* in *chief*, and private *Commanders*, that as our *Royal* Expectation will from henceforward be, to have a ftrict *Account* given us of their careful applying themfelves to the Execution and Obfervance of thefe and all other our *Orders*, with intention of expreffing our fevereft *Difpleafure* againft fuch of them (who- *Strictnefs of Difcipline inculcated, with promife of yet more particular marks of the Kings bounty upon any fignal inftances*

F 2   ever

ever they be) as fhall be found in any
wife negligent or unfaithful in the
fame. So are we no lefs gracioufly
determined at the *End* of their refpective *Voyages*, to Teftifie by fome
efpecial Inftance of our *Bounty* (beyond
what is hereby already fo *Extraordinarily* provided for them) our particular
Regard to whoever of our faid *Commanders* fhall appear to have merited
the fame from us, by any fignal Inftances of their *Induftry, Courage, Conduct*
or *Frugality* evidenced therein on our
behalf. Given at our Court at *Windfor*
this 15*th.* day of *July* 1686.

By his Majefties Command.

S. PEPYS.

*Return to
the Ships.*
𝖂hich Act having been here obferv'd, out of the *Refpect* no lefs due
to the *Care* at the fame time taken
for the *Re-eftablifhment* of good *Gover-
nance* upon his Majefties Ships *abroad*,
than the *Repair* and *Prefervation* of
thofe in *Port*; the Order of thefe
Notes calls for my Return to the
Works

Works in doing upon the latter, and my obferving thereon, as follows, *Viz.*

That the *fatisfaction* his Majefty was pleas'd to conceive from the fore-mentioned *Progrefs* of thefe *Works,* confirm'd by his own frequent *Vifits,* and *Perfonal Infpections* thereinto at the *Yards,* was fuch, as mov'd him (*fix Months* within the time allow'd for it by the *Propofition*) to think them fo far advanc'd, as not to need his any longer continuing the *Sufpenfion* he had for their fakes laid (as before) upon the *Ordinary Methods* of his Navy. And therefore by his great Seal of the 12*th.* of *Octob.* 1688. (after having declar'd his Gracious *Acceptance* and *Approval* of the Services of thefe his *Commiffioners,* in the full Execution of the *Propofition,* and their having brought all matters intrufted to them, into fuch a *Method,* as that his *Officers* might now perform them, more to his *Service,* than formerly they could) He was pleas'd to determine the *Commiffion,*

The Kings fatisfaction in the works done thereon.

From his perfonal Vifits to the Yards, &c.

Octob. 12. 1688. The Execution of the Commiffion approved and confirmed.

He deter-
mines the
Commif-
fion and
recals the
Old Offi-
cers.

Remind
ing them
of their
Old Ac-
counts.

miffion, and recal his faid *Officers* to their ancient *Duties*, according to the known *Inftructions* already in force, and the *Improvements* made therein by thefe *Gentlemen*; inculcating to them his former Directions for the finifhing of their *Accounts*. Among which was in particular that of the *Thirty New Ships*, whereof (but for the *Revolution* immediately following in the *State*) a ftrict *Account* had been foon call'd for, and infifted on by the *King*; as being now (from the through knowledge fince attained concerning them) in a condition of being regularly and effectually controll'd.

Effects of
this Com-
miffion

𝕬𝖓𝖉 fo expir'd this *Commiffion*; and with what *Effects*, in reference to that diverfity of *Services* for which it was Calculated, and (above all) that one of the general Redemption of the *Fleet* of *England* from Ruin, will be

In the
ftate it
then left
the Navy
in.

beft underftood, by looking back to the *State* thereof juft before its open-ing in *January* 168$\frac{5}{6}$, compar'd with what it was left in at this its *Deter-*
mination

mination in *October* 1688. Which latter
follows, *Viz.*

I. The *Fleet* then at *Sea* had (from *Fleet at*
its ordinary *Summer-Guard*) been rais'd *Sea*, *Oct.*
in lefs than two Months (upon intelli- *raifed*
gence of the furprifing Preparations *upon fhort*
then on foot in *Holland*) to no lefs *warning.*
than *fixty feven* of the *King's* own
Ships of *War*, and *Fire-Ships* (befides
Tenders, *Yachts*, and other fmall Im-
barcations) of the Rates following.

Abftract *of the* Fleet *at* Sea *at the*
clofe of the Commiffion *of the*
Navy, October 1688.

Man'd with above 12000 Men.

	N°.	Men.
3*d.* — 12		4715
4 — 28		6318
Rates— 5 — 2		220
6 — 5		370
Fire-Ships — 20		680
Total—67		12303

II. All

Ships in Harbour how re-pair'd.

II. All but *Three* of the whole remaining *Number* (contain'd in the *Propofition*) entirely repair'd, or actually under Repair; with a furplufage of *fix Months* Time, and a fufficiency of *Mony* and *Materials* refting in *Bank* and *Magazine* for compleating that *Remainder.*

Works how per-form'd.

Shewn by the excefs of Charge expended thereon.

III. The *well-performance* of which Works (both for *Extent* and *Subftantial-nefs*) had for its firft *Evidence*, the *Sum* expended thereon, to more by two Thirds than the higheft Value the *Surveyor* of the Navy, and his *Fellow-Officers* had Eftimated, and the *Propo-fition* (grounded on thofe *Eftimates*) Calculated the fame at; divers of them (to above *Thirty*) having been entirely *Rebuilt*, and fome taken up *Hundreds*, others *Thoufands* of Pounds in their *Refitting*, that had but few Months before (without ever going out of *Harbour*) been reprefented by the faid *Officers* to have received from them a *full Repair.*

To which *Proof*, arifing from the

Extra-

Extraordinarinefs of the *Sum* fpent upon *And by*
them, fucceeds that other *Ordinary* one *the Re-*
of the *Reports* of the *Mafter Builders* *ports of*
the Kings
and their *Affiftants*, employ'd in the *Mafter*
Direction, and immediate Supervi- *Builders*
fure thereof. The Names of whom *and Af-*
fiftants.
follow.

A Lift of all his *Majefties* Mafter
Shipwrights and their *Affiftants* ferv-
ing him in his feveral *Yards* between
April 1686. and *October* 1688.

Wherein Note † *fignifies Dead and*
* Preferred.

Yards.	Mr. Shipwrights.	Affiftants.
Chath.	Mr. *Robert Lee*	{ * *Dan. Furzer* *Edw. Dummer* *Phineas Pett*
Portf.	Mr. *Ifaac Betts.*	*Wm. Stiggant*
Dept.	{ † Mr. *John Shifh* Mr. *Fifh. Harding*	* *Fifh. Harding* *Zach. Medbury*
Woolw.	{ † Mr. *Tho. Shifh* Mr. *Jof. Lawrence*	
Sheern.	{ * Mr. *J. Lawrence* Mr. *Dan. Furzer*	

Perfons

Perfons, who (befides their having long before the *Date* of this *Commiffion,* or any occafion fore-feen for it, been from the Credit of their *Abilities* advanc'd to thefe Charges in the time of *K. Charles*) had not only been all

of them employ'd by the *Navy-Officers* themfelves in taking the very *Surveys* upon which the *Eftimates* of the Fleet's Decays were Calculated, and thereby rendred themfelves the moft concern'd to juftifie the fame by fuitable Per-formances thereof, both as to Charge and efficacy; but the **Perfons** upon whofe *Teftimonies,* and theirs only, in right and virtue of their *Places,* under

the *Infpeâion* of the *Surveyor* of the Navy and *Commiffioners* of the Yards (among whom in particular he at *Chatham* was at this time, for the importance of the Works there, one of the firft Form of the *Mafter Builders* of *England*) the Crown always *has,* now *does,* and *for ever muft* depend for its fecurity in this *Matter;* as being (in a word) the **Perfons,** who by the

Prac-

Practice of the *Navy* ſtand *alone charg'd with*, by their *Perſonal* ſervices can *alone* be *knowing Judges of*, and by the ſtanding *Obligations* of their *Places* do therefore *alone* reſt *accountable*, and (as ſuch) are only to be reſorted to by the Crown for its ſatisfaction, in this *Particular*.

IV. Not only the ſix requir'd by the *Propoſition*, but a compleat *Proportion* of eight Months *Sea-Stores* were actually provided and left by theſe *Gentlemen* in *Magazine* (each within its Diſtinct and proper *Repoſitory*) for every Ship ſo repaired; with the like in Materials and Mony for the whole *Remainder*, as faſt as finiſh'd. *Every repaired Ship furniſh'd with 8 Months Sea Stores.*

And not only ſo; but in conſideration of the different and uncertain *Meaſures* by which *Boatſwains* and *Carpenters* of *Ships* had been heretofore ſupply'd (ſometimes too ſparingly with regard to the Kings Service, other whiles too largely with reſpect to his Purſe) they made it their Work (upon beſt Information) to digeſt and ſee *The uncertain Meaſures thereof adjuſted, aſcertain'd, and enlarg'd.*

con-

confirm'd by his *Majesty*, one uniform *Establishment* of *Sea-Stores* for an Officer of each Rate; and that so ample a one, as to be thought sufficient for answering (upon occasion) a yet longer *Expence* than what it was strictly Cal-

Benefit thereof to the King, culated for. So as (to give it in *their* own Terms to the *King* (*We hope your Majesty will from henceforward hear no more of the many Evils attending the former Practice. Especially; if the* Good

Commanders doing their part. Husbandry *of Your* Commanders *shall bear any Proportion to that Mark of* Bounty, *which by your Late* Establishment *you have been pleas'd to grant for their* Encouragement *thereto.*

Besides which Sea-stores to each Ship, a general Magazine is [1] *left, valued together at near* 400000 l. And yet to this so inlarged a Proportion of *Stores* set apart for every particular Ship (and amounting, with them at Sea, to above two hundred and fourscore Thousand pounds) they still added (beyond all *Example*) and left entirely in *Magazine,* such a further *Reserve* for answering the general Service of the *Navy,* as amounted in eight only *Species* thereof, to above

[1] *is add.* S. P.   *one*

one hundred thousand pounds more ; *Commodities* all of greatest importance and least to be depended-upon from the *Market,* as being (save one) all of *Forreign* Growth, *viz.*

Hemp.	*Canvas.*
Pitch.	*Iron.*
Tar.	*Oyle.*
Rosin.	*Wood.*

V. And for the safer keeping and more orderly disposing of this last-mentioned *Treasure,* by preventing the Wastes, Corruption, Imbezlements, and other the manifold mischiefs attending the want of proper and sufficient *Store-Room,* occasion'd by the constant *Growth* of the *Naval* Action of *England,* without suitable inlargements to its other *Accommodations*; More new *Magazines* have (both as to *Dimensions, Contents,* and *Charge*) been erected within the two years and a half of this *Commission,* than had ever been before, by all the *Kings* of *England* put together.

Store-Room, much wanting in the Navy.

Supply'd by new Erections beyond all it ever had before.

VI. Nor

VI. Nor are the foremention'd *Advances* in these works less owing to the *industry* successfully exercised in the improvement of our *Docks*, than in that of the *Magazines*, by bettering the *Old*, and finishing the *New*; to the raising them to the *State* they are now left in, Superiour to all that the *Navy* of *England* ever before knew. And yet not more then its present Occasions call'd for, as not having permitted any one of them to lye unimploy'd two *Tides* together (while in condition for it) within the whole time.

A suitable improvement of the Docks, and not less wanting.

VII. *Four* and *Twenty* of *Seven* and *Twenty* of his Majesty's *Ships* and *Vessels*, come in from *Sea* during this *Commission*, and therefore (as being then abroad) not provided for in the *Proposition*, have been also fully *repair'd* or left actually under *Repair*, furnish'd with like proportion of *Sea-Stores* (as before) without a Penny supply'd out of the Exchequer towards it.

Ships come home, repair'd and stored, though not of the Proposition.

And

And in the doing this, that moſt important (and till now unheard of) *Article* at the Cloſe of the *Propoſition*, relating to the future maintenance of his *Majeſties Fleets* at *Sea* in their whole *Wear* and *Tear*, at *no higher* charge than that of 22 *s. per* Man a Month, has been alſo made good ; and, in that *ſingle* performance, a Foundation laid of ſaving to the Crown for ever, not only the whole *firſt Coſt* of what-ever Ships it shall have occaſion of building in lieu of others become *irre-pairable*; but twenty ſix *per Cent* in the Charge of all ſucceeding Repairs and Expence in their Stores and Furniture.

VIII. Every other Head of the *Pro-poſition* ſtrictly comply'd with, the Building of two ſmall *Frigats* only ex-cepted, which by expreſs Command of the *King* were reſpited (and the Value of them therefore left uncall'd-for out of the *Treaſury*) till the weightier Works of his great *Ships* would allow *Room* and *Leaſure* for their being built in his own Yards.

And this within the Rate in the Propoſi-tion of 22 s. for Wear and Tear.

Saving for ever the whole firſt Coſt of New-building, and 26 per Cent *in all ſuc-ceeding Charges upon the Bodies of the Ships.*

Nothing undone of thePropo-ſition, but two of the ſmall Frigats reſpited by Order.

IX. Not

Not a Penny of Debt un-satisfy'd, where the Party was at hand qualify'd to receive it.
IX. Not a *Penny* left unpaid to any *Officer*, *Seaman*, *Workman*, *Artificer* or *Merchant*, for any *Service* done in, or *Commodity* deliver'd to the use of the *Navy*, either at Sea or on Shore, within the whole time of this *Commission*, where the *Party* claiming the same was in the way to receive it, and had (if an *Accountant*) done his part, as such, towards the entitling himself to Payment.

Even in which Case too, a sufficiency of *Cash* was left in *Bank* upon the Fond of this *Commission*, for clearing that *Debt*, as fast as by the Coming in of *Ships*, and adjustment of *Accounts*, the same could be brought into a *Capacity* and *Right* of being paid.

The Proposition perform-ed and Navy re-deemed, at what Charge.
X. Lastly, The whole of this *Proposition* was thus made good, and therewith the *Navy* of *England* redeem'd from perishing, at a *Charge* not only not exceeding the 400000 *l.* *per Ann.* allotted for it by the *King*, and consequently not more than what the *Navy* appear'd (as before) to have been

been fupply'd with all the time of its being fo abandon'd to *Ruine*, but even for lefs than 310000 l. *per Annum* ; as the fame ftands verify'd by the *Accounts* thereof in the *Regiftry* of the *Navy*, and thofe Accounts (both as to Truth and Perfpicuity (fo digefted, juftify'd, and (after the Clofe of each year) prefented to the *King* and his *Treasurers*, anfwering in every refpect the Scope of the *Propofition*, by diftinct Reckonings exhibited therein of every *Species* and parcel of *Goods* bought and fpent, *Artificer* and *Workman* employ'd, *Penny* laid out, and *Service* perform'd (with the Difference or Agreement in the Charge of every fuch *Service* with its proper *Eftimate*) as does not appear to have ever before been feen in the *Navy* of *England*, but (through the fingle *Induftry* and peculiar *Conduct* of Mr. *Hewer*) is now remaining there, to fhew *Pofterity*, that there is nothing in the *Nature, Bulk*, or *Diverfity* of Matters incident to the bufinefs of a *Navy* (even under the

Verify'd by the Accounts thereof.

circumſtances of *this*) to juſtifie the ſo-long-admitted Pretence of an *Irreducibleneſs* of its *Accounts*, to a degree of *Order* and *Self-Evidence* equal to the moſt ſtrict of any private Merchant.

General State of the Account upon this Propoſition, &c.

The general *State* of which *Accounts* in the Caſe of the preſent *Propoſition*, and the *Works* attending it (as the ſame ariſes from the *ſubordinate Accounts* relative thereto) follows.

Which

A General State of Account, Relating to the 400000. l. per Ann. payable out of the Exchequer to the Treasurer of the Navy, for answering Mr. Pepys's Proposition; As also to other Monies receiv'd, Works done, and Payments made Extraordinary in the Navy, under the Late Commission began March 25. 1685. and Determined October 12. 1688. being two Years, Six Months and two Weeks; according to Particulars verifying the same.

The Exchequer to the Navy is — Dr.

	£.	s.	d.
The Proposition of 400000. l. per Ann., assign'd for the particular Works and Services especially nam'd therein	1015384	12	00

The Excess of Charge in the Repairs of Ships and Vessels beyond the Estimates thereof made by the Officers of the Navy, according to the 2d. Article of the said Proposition. — £. 82870.

The like Excess (according to the 2d. and 3d. Articles of the same) in the Charge of Rigging, and Boatswains and Carpenters Sea-stores beyond their Estimate. — 41016.

Extraordinary Works and Services perform'd in pursuance of special Articles in the said Proposition, nac chargeable upon the 400000.l. viz.

The Value of Wear, and Tear of 24 Ships and Vessels repair'd, equipp'd, and furnish'd with Sea-stores, computed at 22 s. per Man a Month, according to the supplemental Article in the Proposition relating to Ships at Sea upon the 25th. of March 1686. that should come in during this Commission. — 76600.

To fo much upon — 204486 : 00 : 00

Extraordinary Works and Services done by Order, neither provided for, nor mention'd in the Proposition, such as (among others) the Erecting the several Store-houses, and other New-structures in the Yards; the Magazines of Stores, provided for the General service of the Navy, over and above the 8 Months Sea-stores set apart for each Ship; and the Excess of Charge in Victuals and otherwise upon the Ships set out for the Lord Dartmouth's Fleet in August and September 1688, above the 4000 Men provided for in the Proposition, &c. — 178905 : 01 : 07

	£.	s.	d.
From Total	1394775	13	07
Take the Credit-side	1087205	04	03
Exchequer remains Debtor to the Navy upon this Account, over and above the 121291 l. per contra.	307570	09	04

Per Contra — Cr.

	£.	s.	d.
Payd to the Treasurer of the Navy in part of the 1015384. 12. 00, per Contra	849670	0	0

So much left expended in the Repair of several Ships, then they were Estimated at: — £. 1738.

The Value of the Estimates wholly unexpended upon Ships judged irreparable. — 6553.

The Value of the Estimates of three Ships remaining fit to be repaired, viz. — 8128.

Credit to be given this Account, according to the 2d. 3d. and 5th. Articles of the Proposition for — 38076 : 0 : 0

By
	£.
Prince	4719.
Victory	1841.
Royal-Oake	968.
	8128.

The Value of the Hulls of two of the small Frigats forbore to be built by the special Command of His Majesty. — 6000.

More paid to the Treasurer of the Navy in part of the 178905 : 1 : 7. per Contra. — 66167 : 4 : 3

More chargeable on the said Treasurer for the Proceed of several Ships and Vessel fold as decay'd and unserviceable; with other extraordinary sums in further part of the 178905 : 1 : 7 per Contra. — 12000 : 0 : 0

So much left unpay'd by the Commission at the Determination thereof (with its Value le't in the Exchequer upon the Fund of the Proposition or defraying the same), Viz. — 78167 : 4 : 3

Upon
	£.
Wages to the {Ships at Sea	104432.
{Yards	8900.
Bills for Stores Workmanship, &c. unadjusted	8660.
	121291 : 0 : 0

Total — 1087205 : 4 : 3

Which *State* of *Accounts* being (as it ought) admitted, in right to its *Vouchers* now resting (as from the very *Close* of this *Commission* they have done) in the *hands* of the so often-mentioned *Officers* of the *Navy*, who (after what has been here said) cannot but be esteem'd in *Honour* the most concern'd, as well as by *Duty* the most oblig'd, to see the same fully *controll'd*; these (among other *Particulars* no less considerable) offer themselves to Observation, *viz.*

The Officers of the Navy possessed of the Vouchers of this Account, and most concerned to see it controlled.

1. That the 307000 *l.* the *Ballance* of this *Account*, is the *Product* of these Gentlemens *Management*; as being so much saved of what might unexceptionably have been expended by them, out of the 400000 *l. Fond* assigned to the use of this *Proposition*.

Observables from this Account.

307000 l. saved upon the Proposition.

2. That among the several other immediate and important *Fruits* of this *Saveing*, this is one; namely, the obtaining such an Enlargement of *Magazines*, and the amassing therein such a *Treasure* of *Stores*, as *England* was never before *Mistress* of, nor

Fruits of this Saving.

G 2   could

could now have had its *Navy* longer
fupported without.

3. *Laſtly*, That this and all the
above-mentioned *Advantages* have
been effected at no other *Coſt*, than
the bare *Wages* of the few His
Majeſty was pleas'd to call to this
his Service, ariſing together to little
more than 6000 *l.* While (had the
Work been tranſacted by *Contract*) the
whole of that 307000 *l. Ballance* muſt
inconteſtably have been the *Reward*
of the *Undertakers*; and the *Bargain*
neverthelefs not reckon'd any un-
thrifty one to the *Publick*, when it
fhould be conſider'd, that the Execution of this *Propoſition* (with the many
Benefits attending it) within lefs than
three years, would (even with that
Sum included) have barely amounted
to **One** *Million* ; while *five* entire years
were loſt, and the *Navy* all that time
left under little lefs than a total
Deſertion, at the Expence (as before)
of full **Two**. And of that alfo
(without offence be it obſerv'd) near
Five and *thirty thouſand Pounds* taken

up

up in *Wages* only, to a *Commiſſion* of the *Admiralty*, during that very Management; While this appears exempt of the *Charge* of any ſuch *Commiſſion*, or ought elſe extraordinary to the value of a *Shilling*, beyond the Simple *Wages* of a worn unaſſiſted SECRETARY.

And yet with ſuch *Effect* too; that from the *Condition* the *Navy* was (by its own Officers) reported in, at His *Majeſty*'s Reſuming it in 1684, when the *Groſs* of its *Ships* were wholly out of *Repair*, and the beſt of them ready to *ſink* in *Harbour*, with little appearance of its having by this time had any one of them in a *State* of *Service*; it has the preſent *Reputation* (1690) of having *actually* at *Sea* of its own *Ships* of *War* and *Fire-ſhips* (excluſive of *Merchant-men* and *Forreigners*) a *Force* equal at leaſt, or rather ſuperior, to the moſt *powerful* it ever at any one time had, in the moſt *active* year of a *Hollands-War*. And (which is more) the *Reſidue* (as to their *Hulls* and *Stores*) in a ready *State* of following them, if (as I am not to doubt) the
ſame

And the different Effects thereof.

fame *wholefom Methods* have been fince exercis'd towards them, with thofe they were brought-by into the *Condition* this *Commiffion* left them in, upon the 12th of *October*, 1688.

The State of the Fleet in October 1688. *carried on to the Day of the King's withdrawing himfelf in* December.

Which leading me back to the fore-mentioned *State* of this *Affair* in *October*; little refts for the carrying it on to that *fignal Day*, that puts a natural *Bound* to the *fubject* of thefe *Notes*, I mean the *Day* of my late *Royal* (but moft unhappy) *Mafter's* Retiring in *December*; As having received little other *Alteration* within that time, than what arofe from a fmall *Addition* to the *Fleet* under the Lord *Dartmouth*, and the coming home of fome few others from *Forreign Service*; rendering the *whole* then abroad, as follows,

Abftract *of the* Ships *of* War *and* Fire-Ships *in* Sea-Pay *upon the* 18th *of* December, 1688.

Manned with above 14600 Men.

Rate

| | | Ships | | | Men. | Ships at Sea in December 1688. |
		At Sea.	Going out.	Total		
Rate	3d	10	5	15	6080	
	4	29	2	31	7015	
	5	2	0	2	220	
	6	4	0	4	295	
Fire-Ships		22	4	26	965	
Bomber		1	0	1	75	
Total		68	11	79	14650	

𝕿𝖍𝖊 *Import* of which *Fleet*, at a *The fame* *Crifis* fo eminent, as this is likely to *Reported more par-* appear in the future *Annals* of *England* *ticularly,* (when it fhall be remembred what *for the* paffed, befides it, upon the *Britifh-* *fake of* *Seas* between the two laft-cited Periods *what oc-curr'd in* of *October* and *December*) feeming to *our Seas* require fome more diftinct *Report* of *within-* it, than what is to be gathered from *that In terval.* the foregoing *Abftracts*; I fubjoyn a *Lift*, fpecifying the *Rate*, *Name*, *Officers*, *Complement* of *Men* and *Station* of every Ship and Veffel of His *Majefty*'s then in *Sea-Service*, viz.

A

A *General* 𝕷𝖎𝖘𝖙 of all His Majefty's
Pay, upon the 18th of *December*, 1688.
Lieutenants, Complements of *Men,* and

Rates	Ships	Commanders
3d	*Refolution* ——— {	L. *Dartmouth* Ad. C. *Davis* ———
3	*Elizabeth* ——— {	S. *J. Berry* V. Ad. C. *Nevill* ———
3	*Cambridge* ———	C. *Tyrwhit* ———
3	*Defiance* ———	C. *Afhby* ———
3	*Dreadnought* ———	C. *Akarman* ———
3	*Henrietta* ———	C. *Trevanion* ———
3	*Mary* ———	C. *Layton* ———
3	*Pendennis* ———	Sir *Will. Booth*
3	*Plymouth* ———	C. *Carter* ———
3	*York* ———	C. *Delavall* ———
4th	*Advice* ———	C. *Williams* ———
4	*Albans* Saint ———	C. *Conftable* ———
4	*Anthelope* ———	C. *Ridley* ———

Ships and *Veſſels* in *Sea-Service* and 89
with their reſpective *Rates, Commanders,*
Stations.

Lieutenants	Men	Station
{ *Milliſon* ——— { *Preene* ———	450	
{ *Gother* ——— { *Crawley* ———	475	
{ *Wrigh* ——— { *Bois* ———	420	
{ *Bing* ——— { *Littleton* ———	390	
{ *Bounty* ——— { *Tyrwhit* ———	355	
{ *Gardner* ——— { *Dilks* ———	355	
{ *Towneſend* ——— { *Hays* ———	355	} Channel
{ *Jennings* ——— { *Kerr* ———	460	
{ *Foulks* ——— { *Edwards* ———	340	
{ *Moody* ——— { *Manley* ———	340	
Haughton ———	230	
{ *Killigrew* ——— { *Bundee* ———	280	
Pugh ———	230	

Rates	Ships	Commanders
4th	*Aſſurance*	C. *Mack Donell.*
4	*Bonadventure*	C. *Hopſon*
4	*Briſtoll*	C. *Leighton*
4	*Centurion*	C. *Elliot*
4	*ConſtantWarwick*	C. *Cornwall*
4	*Crown*	C. *Robinſon*
4	*David* Saint	C. *Botham*
4	*Deptford*	C. *Rook*
4	*Diamond*	C. *Walters*
4	*Dover*	C. *Shovel*
4	*Foreſight*	C. *Standley*
4	*Greenwich*	C. *Wrenn*
4	*Jerſey*	C. *Beverly*
4	*Mordaunt*	C. *Tyrrell*
4	*New Caſtle*	C. *Churchill*
4	*Nonſuch*	C. *Montgomery*
4	*Phœnix*	C. *Gifford*
4	*Portland*	C. *G. Aylemore*
4	*Portſmouth*	C. St. *Loe*
4	*Ruby*	C. *Froud*
4	*Swallow*	C. *M. Aylemore*
4	*Tiger*	C. *Tennant*

Lieutenants	Men	Station
Fitz Patrick———	180	
Granvil———	230	
{*Penn*———	230	
Townfend——}		
	230	
Hales———	180	
Wickham———	230	
{*Jennings*———	280	
Walker——}		
{*Guy*———	280	
Bowyer——}		
Greenway———	230	Channel
Dawes———	230	
{*Hubbard*———	230	
Man——}		
{*Vaughan*———	280	
Audeley——}		
Hammond———	230	
Carveth———	230	
Harman———	280	
Talbot———	180	
Harrifon———	180	
Trevanion———	240	
Beaumont———	220	
Gillam———	230	
Whittaker———	230	
L. *Will. Murray*	230	

Rates	Ships	Commanders
4th	*Woolwich*———	C. *Haſtings*———
6	*Lark*———	C. *Grimſditch*—
6	*Saudados*———	C. *Graydon*———
Bomb.	*Fire Drake*———	C. *Leake*———
Ketch	*Quaker*———	C. *Allin*———
Yts.	*Cleveland*———	C. *Hoskins*———
	Fubbs———	C. *R. Sanderſon*
	Iſabella———	C. *W. Sanderſon*
	Katherine———	C. *Clements*———
	Kitchin———	C. *Crow*———
	Mary———	C. *Fazeby*———
F.Sh.	*Cygnet*———	C. *Shelley*———
	Dartmouth———	C. *Legg*———
	Elizab and *Sarah*	C. *Dover*———
	Guardland———	C. *Jenifer*———
	Richard & John—	C. *Will Wright*
	Supply———	C. *Croſſe*———
	Guernſey———	C. *Arthur*———
	Pearl———	C. *Coale*———
	Richmond———	C. *Fairborne*—
	Swan———	C. *Johnſon*———
	Sophia———	C. *Mings*———
	Speedwell———	C. *Powſon*———
	Roſe Salley Prize	
	Saint *Paul*———	C. *Boteler*———
	Charles & Henry	C. *Stone*———

Lieutenants	Men	Station
{ *Talmach*——— } { *Baker*——— }	280	
	85	
	75	
	75	
	40	
	30	
	40	
	30	
	30	
	30	
	30	
	30	
	55	Channel
	25	
	50	
	20	
	20	
	50	
	50	
	50	
	50	
	27	
	30	
	37	
	50	
	25	

Rate	Ships	Commanders
F.Sh. {	*Roebuck*	C. *Pooley*
	Unity	C. *Wyvel*
	Charles	C. *Potter*
	Half-moon	C. *Munden*
	Young Spragg	C. *Wiseman*
Yacht	*Merlin*	C. *Wilde*
F.Sh. {	*Eagle*	C. *Willford*
	Sampson	C. *Harris*
Yacht	*Navy*	C. *Cotton*
Ketch	*Kingfisher*	C. *Swaine*
Yacht	*Monmouth*	C. *Will.Wright*
4th	*Dragon*	C. *Killigrew*
4	*Sedgemore*	C. *Lloyd*
5	*Saphire*	C. *Tosier*
Hulk	*Leopard*	
4	*Assistance*	C. *Law.Wright*
6	*Drake*	C. *Spragg*
5	*Rose*	C. *George*
Ketch	*Deptford*	C. *Berry*
6	*Dunbarton*	C. *Roe*

Lieutenants	Men	Station	
	16	} Channel	
	25		
	30		
	35		
	20	} *Portſm.*	} Guard
	30		
	45	} *Sheern.*	
	50		
	20	*Guernſey*	
	15	*Jerſey*	
	20	*Ireland*	
{*Bokenham*— *Sherborne*—}	185	} *Salley*	
{*Buckely*— *Hawkins*—}	240		
Brisbane—	115		
	33		
Chapman—	200	} *Jamaica*	
	65		
Condon—	105	*New-England*	
	40	} *Virginia*	
	70		

Ships

Ships just come-in		
Rate	Ships	Commanders
3d	Montague———	L.Berkley,R.Ad.
3	Rupert———	Sir Will Jennens

Ships go-		
Rate	Ships	Commanders
3d	Edgar———	L.Berkley,R.Ad.
3	Dunkirk———	
3	Warspight———	Sir Will Jennens
3	Hampton-Court—	C. Priestman—
3	Kent———	Sir F. Wheeler-
4	Tiger Prize———	C. Smith———
4	Sweepstakes ——	
F. Sh. {	Mermaid———	C. Ley———
	Thomas & Eliz.	
	Owners Love———	
	Cadiz Merchant--	

Lieutenants	Men	Station
Conway——— Every——— Staggins——— Day———	355 400	Channel.

ing out.

Lieutenants	Men	Station
Every———	460	
———	340	
———	420	
Buck———	460	
Usher———	460	Channel.
Foules———	230	
———	80	
———	50	
———	40	
———	40	
———	45	

Abſtract
of the preceding Liſt

Rates and Qualities	Ships			Men
	At Sea	Going out	Total	
Rates { 3d—	10	5	15	6080
4—	29	2	31	7015
5—	2	0	2	220
6—	4	0	4	295
Fireſhips—	22	4	26	965
Bomber—	1	0	1	75
Hulk—	1	0	1	33
Ketches—	3	0	3	95
Yachts—	9	0	9	260
Total—	81	11	92	15038

And

And to the end nothing may be *A Gen-* wanting to render thefe *Notes* com- *eral Lift* pletely expreffive of the *State*, not of *and State* that *Fleet* only, but of the whole *of the* *whole* Navy of *England* at this fo extra- *Navy of* ordinary *Conjuncture*, I add one *Table* *England,* more, fhewing (through all the prin- *Decem-* cipal¹ *Circumftances* of it) the particular *ber 18,* *Condition*, wherein every *Ship* and *1688.* *Veffel* thereof then ftood, with the united *Force* of the *Whole*, as follows, *viz.*

principal] principle *ed.*

A
LIST and STATE
OF THE
ROYAL NAVY

A

A 𝕷ift and

Of the whole Royal Navy of
Harbour) upon the 18. day of
dition of each *Ship* and *Veffel*
pairs and the Value of their
day; containing alfo an *Account*
prefented to his *Majefty* by the
of every *Ship* comprehended
par'd with the *Real Charge* of the
late *Commiffioners* of the *Navy*,
Commiffion March 25th. 1686. and

Wherein to

That the *Ships* $\begin{cases} \text{Mark'd} \begin{cases} A. \text{ were at } Sea \\ B. \text{ were in } Har\text{-} \\ C. \text{ have been} \end{cases} \\ \text{in the } 𝕭𝖑𝖆𝖈𝖐 \text{ Letter are} \end{cases}$

State

England (whether at *Sea* or in
December 1688. fhewing the *Con-*
therein, with refpect to their *Re-*
Rigging and *Sea Stores,* upon that
of the laft and higheft *Eſtimates*
Officers of his *Navy* of the *Defects*
within *Mr. Pepys's Propoſition* ; com-
Works perform'd. thereon by the
between the *Commencement* of their
its *Determination October* 12. 1688.

be noted,

upon———————————) the faid 25
bour wanting repair, on—— } of *March*
added to the *R. Navy,* fince) 1686.
the 30 *New Ships.*

Ships

Ships and Vessels.	Place and Condition		
	At Sea or going forth.	In Har-	
		re-pair'd.	Under Repair.
1ft. Rate.			
St. Andrew———	B ——	*	
Brittannia———	B ——		*
Charles Royal—	B ——	*	
George St.———	B ——		*
James Royal——	B ——	*	
London———	B ——	*	
Michael St.———	B ——		*
Prince Royal—	B ——		
Soveraign———	B ——	*	
2d. Rate.			
Albemarle———	B ——	*	
Coronation———	B ——	*	
Duke———	B ——	*	
Dutchefs———	B ——	*	
Katherine———	B ——		*
Neptune ———	B ——	*	
Oflory ———	B ——	*	

bour.		Estimates of their Defects.	Real charge of their Repairs.	Value of their Rigging and Sea Stores.
To be re-pair'd.	Newly come in from Sea.			
		£.	£.	£.
		1616	1650	4296
		2315	2138	5181
		1577	1646	4735
		1918	———	4296
		1400	1882	4735
		796	1574	4296
		1286	5092	3668
*		———		4735
		2134	1349	5181
		13042	15331	41123
		3213	3773	4296
		1200	1327	4296
		719	2862	4296
		1193	2826	4296
		1499	2081	3668
		949	1622	4296
		837	745	4296

Ships and Veſsels.	Place and Condition		
	At Sea or going forth.	In Har-	
		re-pair'd.	Under Repair.
Sandwich———	B		*	
Vanguard———	B		*	
Victory———	B			
Windſor Caſtle —	B		*	
3d. Rate.				
Anne ———	B		*	
Berwick———	B		*	
Bredah———	B		*	
Burford———	B		*	
Cambridge———	B	*		
Captain———	B		*	
Defiance———	B	*		
Dreadnought——	B	*		
Dunkirk———	B	*		
Eagle———	B		*	
Edgar———	B	*		
Elizabeth———	B	*		

Dec. 18. 1688.				
bour.		Estimates of their Defects.	Real charge of their Repairs.	Value of their Rigging and Sea Stores.
To be re-pair'd.	Newly come in from Sea.			
		£.	£.	£.
___	___	1622	3015	4296
		897	1027	4296
*	-----			3668
___	___	650	3438	4296
		12779	22716	46000
___	___	862	2203	2976
___	___	1055	370	2976
___	___	1186	1742	2976
___	___	975	2165	2976
___	___	944	4999	2580
___	___	1215	3046	2976
___	___	512	1747	2365
___	___	1140	1780	2195
___	___	409	592	1903
___	___	705	586	2976
___	___	1911	7141	2976
___	___	503	1444	2976

Ships and Vessels.	Place and Condition		
	At Sea or going forth.	In Har-	
		re-pair'd.	Under Repair.
Essex	B		*	
Exeter	B		*	
Expedition	B		*	
Grafton	B		*	
Hampt. Court	B	*		
Harwich	B		*	
Henrietta	B	*		
Hope	B		*	
Kent	B	*		
Lenox	B		*	
Lion	B		*	
Mary	B	*		
Monck	B			*
Monmouth	B		*	
Montague	B		*	
Northumberl.	B		*	
Royal Oak	B			
Pendennis	B	*		
Plymouth	B	*		
Resolution	B	*		

bour.		Estimates of their Defects.	Real charge of their Repairs.	Value of their Rigging and Sea Stores.
To be re-pair'd.	Newly come in from Sea.			
		£.	£.	£.
		1427	1454	2976
		1391	553	2976
		725	401	2976
		735	1496	2976
		830	4771	2976
		634	885	2580
		594	945	2195
		1257	1922	2976
		1382	1670	2976
		354	797	2976
		602	955	2195
		3152	7236	2195
		1565	2212	2195
		997	5643	2365
		503	3814	2365
		1186	1114	2976
*				2976
		736	1521	2976
		670	1111	2195
		510	1292	2365

Ships and Vessels.	Place and Condition		
	At Sea or going forth.	In Har- *re-pair'd.*	In Har- *Under repair.*
𝕽eſtauration	B	*	
Rupert	B	*	
𝕾terling=Caſt.	B	*	
𝕾uffolk	B	*	
Swiftſure	B	*	
Warſpight	B	*	
York	B	*	
4th. Rate.			
Advice	B	*	
Albans St.	C	*	
Anthelope	B	*	
Aſſiſtance	B	*	
Aſſurance	B	*	
Bonadventure	A	*	
Briſtol	A	*	
Charles Gally	B		
Centurion	B	*	

Dec. 18. 1688. bour.		Estimates of their Defects.	Real charge of their Repairs.	Value of their Rigging and Sea Stores.
To be re-pair'd.	Newly come in from Sea.			
		£.	£.	£.
		2969	734	2976
		129	420	2365
		1349	2033	2976
		357	1857	2976
		610	941	2580
		1959	4130	2365
		1460	4147	2165
		39502	81869	104670
		2902	1558	1582
		2212	3597	1582
		1749	2142	1582
		1812	3640	1582
		989	1316	1348
				1582
				1582
	*	186	183	1348
		1222	3498	1582

Ships and Vessels.		Place and Condition		
		At Sea or going forth.	In Har-	
			re-pair'd.	Under Repair.
Conſtant Warwick	B	*		
Crown	A	*		
David St.	B	*		
Deptford	C	*		
Diamond	B	*		
Dover	B	*		
Dragon	B	*		
Faulcon	A			
Foreſight	B	*		
Greenwich	B	*		
Hampſhire	B		*	
Happy Return	A			*
James Gally	A		*	
Jerſey	B	*		
King-fiſher	A			*
Mary Roſe	A			
Mary Gally	C		*	
Mordaunt	B	*		
New Caſtle	B	*		
Nonſuch	B	*		

Dec. 18. 1688.

bour.		Estimates of their Defects.	Real charge of their Repairs.	Value of their Rigging and Sea Stores.
To be re-pair'd.	Newly come in from Sea.			
		£.	£.	£.
		1189	451	1348
		—	—	1582
		210	687	1903
	—	2377	4596	1728
		576	821	1582
		1849	3043	1582
		748	268	1472
	*	—	—	1348
		390	380	1582
		280	374	1903
		2500	3349	1472
		—	—	1728
		—	—	1348
		2254	1416	1582
		—	—	1903
	*	—	—	1582
		—	—	1348
		642	1025	1582
		1329	2223	1728
		1721	2024	1348

Ships and Veſſels.	At Sea or going forth.	In Har[bour]	
		re-pair'd.	Under Repair.
Oxford ——— A			*
Phœnix——— A	*		
Portland——— B	*		
Portſmouth——— B	*		
Reſerve——— B			
Ruby ——— A	*		
Sedgemore ——— C	*		
Swallow——— B	*		
Sweepſtakes——— B	*		
Tiger——— B	*		
Tiger Prize——— B	*		
Woolwich——— B	*		
5th. Rate.			
Roſe——— A	*		
Saphire——— A	*		

Dec. 18. 1688. bour.		Eſtimates of their Defects.	Real charge of their Repairs.	Value of their Rigging and Sea Stores.
To be re-pair'd.	Newly come in from Sea.	£.	£.	£.
		—	—	1903
		—	—	1348
		1922	4689	1728
		2500	2649	1472
	*	427	259	1582
				1582
		2337	3650	1728
		1314	1571	1582
		1368	1612	1348
		326	365	1728
		1348	1102	1582
		525	1513	2195
		39204	54001	65199
		—	—	902
		—	—	1031
				1933

Ships and Vessels.		Place and Condition		
		At Sea or going forth.	In Har[bour] re-pair'd.	Under Repair.
6th. Rate.				
Drake————	A	*		
Dunbarton——	B	*		
Fanfan———	B		*	
Greyhound——	A		*	
Larke———	A	*		
Saudados ——	A	*		
Bombers				
Fire-Drake——	C	*		
Portſmouth——	A		*	
Salamander——	C		*	
Fire Ships				
Cadiz-Merchant—	C	*		
Cygnet———	C	*		
Charles———	C	*		

Dec. 18. 1688.				
bour.		Estimates of their Defects.	Real charge of their Repairs.	Value of their Rigging and Sea Stores.
To be re-pair'd.	Newly come in from Sea.			
		£.	£.	£.
				536
—	—	156	288	634
—	—	30	36	391
—	—			634
—	—			634
—	—			634
		186	324	3463
—	—			634
—	—			391
—	—			536
				1561
—	—			250
—	—			250

Ships and Veſſels.		Place and Condition		
		At Sea or going forth.	In Har	
			re-pair'd.	Under Repair.
Charles and Henry	C	∗		
Dartmouth———	A	∗		
Eagle———	A	∗		
Eliz. and Sarah.-	C	∗		
Guardland———	B	∗		
Guernſey———	B	∗		
Half-Moon———	C	∗		
Mermaid———	A	∗		
Owners Love———	C	∗		
Pearle———	A	∗		
Paul St.———	B	∗		
Rich. and John —	C	∗	—	
Richmond———	B	∗		
Roebuck———	C	∗		
Roſe———	B	∗		
Sampſon———	B	∗		
Sophia———	B	∗		
Speedwell———	C	∗		
Supply———	C	∗		
Swann———	B	∗		

Dec. 18. 1688.				
bour.		Estimates of their Defects.	Real charge of their Repairs.	Value of their Rigging and Sea Stores.
To be re-pair'd.	Newly come in from Sea.			
		£.	£.	£.
		—	—	273
		—	—	1031
		—	—	902
		—	—	300
		295	147	1031
		1150	1685	1031
		—	—	634
		—	—	1031
		—	—	1031
		630	1014	1031
		590	1403	902
		—	—	250
		155	575	902
		520	411	902
		110	182	536
		—	—	280
		795	633	1031

Ships and Vessels.		Place and Condition		
		At Sea or going forth.	In Har	
			re-pair'd.	Under Repair.
Thomas and Eliz.	C	*	—	—
Unity———	C	**	—	—
Young Spragg—	B	*	—	—
Hoys.				
Delight———	B	—	*	—
Lighter———	B	—	*	—
Marygold———	B	—	*	—
Nonsuch———	C	—	*	—
Transporter———	B	—	*	—
Unity Horseboat-	B	—	*	—
Hulkes.				
Arms of Horne—	B	—	*	—
Arms of Rotterd.-	B	—	*	—
French Ruby———	B	—	*	—
George Saint———	B	—	*	—

Dec. 18. 1688.		Estimates of their Defects.	Real charge of their Repair.	Value of their Rigging and Sea Stores.
bour.				
To be re-pair'd.	Newly come in from Sea.	£.	£.	£.
				277
		80	126	390
		4325	6176	14265
		129	83	—
		2065	680	—
		1427	193	—

Ships and Vessels.	Place and Condition		
	At Sea, or going forth.	In Har[bour]	
		re-pair'd.	Under Repair.
Leopard —————— B	*		
Maria Prize ——— C	} Gibr.		
Puntoone ———— B			
State-House ——— B		*	
Ketches.			
Deptford ———— A	*		
Kingfisher ——— A	*		
Quaker ————— A	*		
Smacks.			
Escape Royal——— B		*	
Little London —— B		*	
Sheerness ———— B		*	
Shish———————— B		*	
Tow-Engine——— B		*	

Dec. 18. 1688.				
bour.		Estimates of their Defects.	Real charge of their Repairs.	Value of their Rigging and Sea Stores.
To be re-pair'd.	Newly come in from Sea.			
		£.	£.	£.
		3858	1156	1562
		300	126	——
		7779	2238	1562
		——	——	391
		——	——	391
		——	——	391
				1173

Ships and Vessels.		Place and Condition		
		At Sea or going forth.	In Har	
			re-pair'd.	Under Repair
Yachts.				
Charlotte———	A		*	
Cleveland———	B	*		
Fubbs———	A	*		
Henrietta———	A		*	
Jemmy———	B		*	
Isabella———	A	*		
Isle of Wight——	B		*	
Katherine———	A	*		
Kitchin———	A	*		
Mary———	A	*		
Merlin———	B	*		
Monmouth ——	A	*		
Navy———	A	*		
Quinborow———	B		*	

Dec. 18. 1688.		Estimates of their Defects.	Real charge of their Repair.	Value of their Rigging and Sea Stores.
bour.				
To be re-pair'd.	Newly come in from Sea.			
		£.	£.	£.
		———	———	550
		———	———	550
		———	———	550
		———	———	550
		———	———	160
		———	———	360
		———	———	100
		———	———	550
		———	———	500
		———	———	550
		———	———	550
		———	———	550
		———	———	400
		———	———	50
				5970

An Abſtract of the foregoing *Liſt* England, upon the 18. of *December*			
	Place and *Condition*		
Ships and Veſſels.	*At Sea or going forth.*	In Har	
		re- pair'd.	*Under Repair.*
Rates { 1.—		5	3
2.—		9	1
3.—	15	22	1
4.—	31	3	3
5.—	2		
6.—	4	2	
Bombers——	1	2	
Fireſhips——	26		
Hoys——		6	
Hulks——	1	7	
Ketches——	3		
Smacks——		5	
Yachts——	9	5	
	92	66	8

and *State* of the *Royal Navy* of
1688. with the *Force* of the whole.

127

| *Dec.* 18. 1688. | | | *Force.* | |
| bour. | | | | |
To be re-pair'd.	Newly come in from Sea.	*Total.*	*Men.*	*Guns.*
I	———	9	6705	878
I	———	11	7010	974
1	———	39	16545	2640
———	4	41	9480	1908
———	———	2	260	60
———	———	6	420	90
———	———	3	120	34
———	———	26	905	218
———	———	6	22	———
———	———	8	50	———
———	———	3	115	24
———	———	5	18	———
———	———	14	353	104
3	4	173	42003	6930

Conclufion.

And having thus fummarily brought this *Deduction* of the laft *Ten* years *Home-Tranfactions* of our *Navy* to the day I firft fet for its *Period*, as it alfo (moft wellcomely) proves to my own (now 30 *Years*) Relation to't; wherein (as an *Englifhman*, and in a *Service* purely *Englifh*) I have ever with all fimplicity of mind contended, to render this humble *Province* of mine ufeful to my *Country:* I clofe this **Paper**.

Which amounting to little more than the *Contents* of one *Chapter* of a greater Number, wherewith the *World* may fome time or other be more largely entertain'd upon the general Subject of the *Navalia* of *England*; I have, (for preventing either others or my own being mifled, to the *believing* or *reporting* ought herein needing *Animadverfion*) chofen to expofe what is here faid, Now, while

while fo many are furviving, whofe *Memories* (joyn'd with the eafie Recourfe to be ftill had to the *Original Regifters* thereof in the *Offices* of the *Admiralty* and *Navy*) may enable them to do right to the *Publick*, *Themfelves*, and *Me*, by a timely rectifying of any *Errors*, or Improvement of any *Truths*, which *Time* may otherwife render in themfelves lefs difcoverable, or Us lefs folicitous in the looking after them. In which confideration I fhall (not gladly only, but) thankfully receive Intimations of any *Matters* herein calling for *Amendment*; as wellknowing how far from *infallible* his beft *endeavours* muft be, that has to do with a *Subject* so extenfive, various, and complicate, as that of a *Navy*; and a *Navy* circumftanc'd as this happens to be within the limits of this *Chapter*.

But whatever (more or lefs) I may meet with from better *Hands* towards the improvement of this *Schitz*: Somewhat (I truft) of prefent utility may (even as it is) be hoped for from it, in the fo ample, frefh, and coftly *Experiment* (and to *England* moft inftructive) which this *Paper* exhibits, of the *Validity* of thefe three *Truths* in its *Sea Oeconomy,* Viz.

Corol-   1.——**That** Integrity, *and general*
larys from (*but unpractic'd*) Knowledge, *are not alone*
the Pre- *fufficient to conduct and fupport a* Navy
mifes. *fo, as to prevent its* Declenfion *into a* State *little lefs unhappy, than the worft that can befall it under the* want *of* both.

2.——**That** *not much more* (*neither*) *is to be depended on, even from* Experience *alone and* Integrity ; *unaccompany'd with* Vigour *of* Application, Affiduity, Affection, Strictnefs *of* Difcipline, *and* Method.

3.——**That** *it was a ftrenuous* Conjunction *of all thefe* (*and that* Conjunction *only*) *that within half the* Time, *and lefs than half the* Charge *it coft the* Crown *in the expofing it,* had (*at the very inftant of its unfortunate* Lord's *Withdrawing from it*) rais'd *the* Navy
of

of England *from the lowest state of* Impotence, *to the most advanced step towards a lasting and solid* Prosperity, *that* (*all* Circumstances *consider'd*) *this* Nation *had ever seen it at.*

And yet not such; but that (even at this its *Zenith*) it both did and suffer'd sufficient to *teach* us, that there is *Something* above both *That* and *Us,* that Governs the *World.*

To which (Incomprehen-fible) *alone be*
GLORY.

FINIS.

Index.

A

Index.

Index.

Docks

Index.

D

Docks *Improv'd and Encreas'd.* 77, 78

E

Eaſt-Country $\left\{ \begin{array}{l} \textit{Timb..} \\ \textit{Plank} \end{array} \right\}$ *vide* Plank.

F

Fleet—*Vide*—Ships.

K

King Charles II. *Alters the Method of the* Admiralty. 1

———*By a* Commiſſion *on that behalf* May 1679. 6

———Reſumes *it into his own Hands,* May 1684. 7

———*Dies* February 168⅘. 13

——— James II. *Succeeding applies himſelf to the* Redreſs *of the* Navy. ibid.

———*His* Choice *of* New *Hands.* 26

———Commiſſion *for the* Navy, *April* 1686. 31

———*Enquiries into the* Diſorders *thereof.* 56

———*Perſonal*

Index.

Index.

Index.

Index.

Index.

Store-

Index.

Index.

FINIS.